To Benda –

~~Someone who li~~ Children and has the patience to work with them like you do, will certainly enjoy reading this book.

Love,
Andy

D0935849

Children of Dreams, Children of Hope

Other books by David Melton:

Todd — Prentice-Hall, 1968
I'll Show You the Morning Sun — Stanyon-Random House,
   1971
Judy - A Remembrance — Stanyon-Random House, 1972
When Children Need Help! — Thomas Y. Crowell, 1972
This Man - Jesus — McGraw-Hill, 1972
Burn the Schools - Save the Children — Thomas Y. Crowell,
   1975
And God Created. . . — Herald House, 1975

Children of Dreams, Children of Hope

Raymundo Veras, M.D.
with David Melton

HENRY REGNERY COMPANY · CHICAGO

Library of Congress Cataloging in Publication Data
Veras, Raymundo.
    Children of dreams, children of hope.

    1. Mongolism — Rehabilitation. 2. Brain-damaged
children — Rehabilitation. 3. Philadelphia. Institutes
for the Achievement of Human Potential. 4. Doman,
Glenn J. I. Melton, David, joint author. II. Title.
RJ506.M6V47   1975   362.7'8'3   75-15671
ISBN 0-8092-8384-0

Copyright © 1975 by David Melton and Raymundo Veras
All rights reserved
Published by Henry Regnery Company
180 North Michigan Avenue, Chicago, Illinois 60601
Manufactured in the United States of America
Library of Congress Catalog Card Number: 75-15671
International Standard Book Number: 0-8092-8384-0

Published simultaneously in Canada by
Fitzhenry & Whiteside Limited
150 Lesmill Road
Don Mills, Ontario M3B 2T5
Canada

To my wife, Lourdes —
   with my love.
      I am eager to hand this book to you.

To my son, ZeCarlos,
   and my daughter, Lourdinha —
      you fill my heart with pride and joy.

To Glenn Doman —
   who saved my son's life
      and continues to save the lives of other hurt children.

And to the parents and children —
   their courage and their wisdom
      long ago won my respect and admiration.

Contents

Foreword

Sometimes I think that I am the luckiest of men because I have had the good fortune to meet many of my personal heroes and have been allowed to walk among giants. Dr. Raymundo Veras stands several inches shorter than I—but those inches are only physical measurements. Giants are not gauged by yardsticks alone. In both courage and dedication he towers head and shoulders above most men.

When we began this writing, I envisioned our composing an epic autobiography because Dr. Veras's life has been lived in epic proportions. The first morning I set up a tape recorder and began asking him about his childhood in a small farming village in northern Brazil. I learned that he was one of eighteen children and that, as a young man, he became a renowned ophthalmological surgeon. For over two hours he answered my questions. Then suddenly he stopped.

"Why do you ask me these things about my youth?" he wanted to know.

"For the book," I answered.

"*This* book?"

"Yes," I replied, trying to explain that his colorful background would fascinate the reader.

"Dave," he said, in emphatically determined tones that I shall never forget, "if we write a book about my boyhood, it would please my uncle and my brothers and sisters very much. But I have no time for such writing. This book is not for my family. It is for the parents of mongoloid children. We will not insult them with telling the history of my first life. We tell them how I learn to make mongoloids well. Do you understand?"

I quickly answered, "Yes." Dr. Veras rarely sets his Brazilian jaw, but when he does, few men would dare attempt to argue. Fewer still would win. And, of course, in this case, he was right.

However, though Dr. Veras chose to pass over several aspects of his life in the main body of the book, I feel some of them should be revealed here.

Dr. Veras graduated from the Medical School, University of Bahia, Brazil, in 1937, and was associated with the Public Health Department of Rio de Janeiro from 1938 to 1941 when he was appointed Clinic Chief of the General Hospital of Guanabara State. During World War II, he served as Captain with the Brazilian Army in Italy and was awarded a *Campaign Medal* in 1944. After the war, he became a highly successful opthalmological surgeon.

In 1957 he studied at The Institutes for the Achievement of Human Potential in Philadelphia for one year, and returned to South America to found The Institutes for the Achievement of Human Potential of Brazil, the Centro de Reabilitacao Nossa Senhora de Gloria, Rio de Janeiro. He is currently Medical Director of units located in São Paulo, State of São Paulo; Salvador, State of Bahia; Barbacena, State of Minas Gerais; Porto Alegre, State of Rio Grande do Sul; Sao Lourenco, State of Minas Gerais. He is Scientific Director and Supervisor of the Rehabilitation Center at Peru and The Institute for Neurological Organization, Buenos Aires, Argentina, Medical Supervisor of the Institute for Neurological Organization, Caracas, Venezuela, and Scientific Supervisor of the Institute Maria Jose, Petropolis, Brazil. He is also a member of the Board of Trustees, University of Plano, Texas, and served as President of the International Forum for Neurological Organization.

In 1962, Dr. Veras was awarded the Statue with Pedestal from the International Forum; in 1967, the Golden Liberty Bell; and, in the same year, was granted the title of Honorary Citizen of Dallas, Texas. In 1974, he was elected International President of the World Organization for Human Potential.

The greatness of this man, however, is not measured by medals and awards. The true measure of his achievements lie in his professional genius and in his personal concern for hurt children and their parents. Would that all doctors followed his example. Would that all people felt such concern.

During this writing, Dr. Veras was quite ill. Years of twenty-hour days and very little rest had taken their toll. Yet, as our work progressed, he seemed charged with new energies, and the gaiety that flowed from my studio seemed to touch every corner of our house. He fondly called my wife, Nancy, and our children, Todd and Teresa, his Kansas City family and our house his Kansas City home.

As we neared the completion of the manuscript for this book, Dr. Veras said to me, "I want that my book should have two forewords. I want Glenn Doman to write the first one and you to write the second." (As the reader will later see, Glenn has written an afterword).

I considered his request an honor and immediately a thousand images and thoughts flashed through my mind. There was so much I would like to say about this man and his dedication to make hurt children well. I think Dr. Veras felt that my sudden silence may have indicated that I was at a loss for words.

"It does not have to be long — very short," he said. "You might just say that we are good friends, that we are both fathers, and that we know each other's sons."

I am always touched by his ability to reduce complex relationships to simple statements.

Raymundo Veras and I are good friends. We are both fathers. And we know each other's sons.

His is not a book of history. It is not a book of past reflections. It is a book of exciting new ideas and innovations, which reaches into the future to take its proper place.

David Melton
December 22, 1974

Introduction

This is a simple book.

It is simple not by coincidence, but by design.

It is simple because the truths it contains are simple.

It is simple because I write it in English and not in my native language.

It is simple because it is not written for medical doctors. Often, books written by medical doctors for other medical doctors are filled with sixteen-letter words of professionalism. I am not opposed to such books, nor am I opposed to medical doctors writing such books, but I have no desire to write them.

The main reason I do not write for medical doctors is that they are too slow to respond to new ideas. They read very little, and when they do, too often they say little more than, "Isn't that interesting?" Then they turn over and go to sleep. After twenty or thirty years they gradually accept a new idea and calmly say, "It's not new, but an old proven fact."

Parents of hurt children don't have twenty years to spare

because every day—indeed every minute—they see their child grow older. If they read or hear about a new medical discovery, they cannot turn over and sleep—they get up and anxiously walk the floor, hoping beyond hope that they have found the answer that will make their child well. It is sad that the professional begins to change his mind only after public opinion becomes so strong that he is forced to consider new ideas.

So I write to parents because I have found their thinking to be uncluttered by past misconceptions and opinions. Their goals are clear and well defined. If parents have a hurt child, their first goal is to make that child well. That is a good goal. It is an understandable goal. It is an admirable goal.

Parents are emotional about the welfare of their children and therefore are often called unrealistic. I do not believe that one necessarily leads to the other. In truth, I would think it unrealistic if parents had no emotions for their children or did not feel the urgency to make their children well. If, in their emotional urgency, parents are not willing to wait for thirty years for new medical answers, this should not come as a surprise to physicians. Nor should such attitudes be labeled as unrealistic.

In truth, I think it is often the professional attitudes that are unrealistic, because professional people are frequently prone to become accustomed to sickness. Perhaps that is one of the world's major medical problems—the professionals become involved in labeling and sorting degrees of illness instead of thinking in terms of wellness. If they think their task is to make people less ill or to be content in their illness, they have lost sight of the most important objective and that is, of course, to make the patient well.

As a doctor, I sympathize with the physician. But as a human being, I must ally myself with the goals of parents, because I can better understand their goals. I can better feel their emotions.

This book is in two sections. The first section tells how I learned what I know about mongoloids. The second section tells how it is possible to make mongoloids well.

If you are a parent of a mongoloid child, you may be tempted to skip the first section and turn instead to the last part. Don't do this, for if you read only the last half, you may not completely understand what I tell you. However, if you read only the last half of this book and you make your child well, I forgive you. But if you read only the last half, and because you misunderstand it you do *not* make your child well, I feel only a great sadness for both you and your child.

So be patient and read both sections. I promise you will meet many interesting people and will be introduced to many exciting and new ideas.

Please, if it happens that you are not a parent of a mongoloid child, pretend that you are as you read these pages, so you can feel the urgency of these words.

Children of Dreams, Children of Hope

Part 1

1

The Last Day of
My First Life

I believe in fate.

That does not mean that I am a superstitious man who kisses the feet of idols. It only means that I have lived long enough to become aware that there are forces that suddenly confront us and events that have the power to change our lives forever.

I know this is true because I have faced such a moment, an event, which in a segment of time took only seconds but its force touched my family with such impact that from that moment on, our lives have never again been the same.

In 1957, my life seemed to be set, and there was a certain rhythm in my days. I was an ophthalmological surgeon who had gained some respect and notoriety in Rio de Janeiro. Financially, I was a little better than secure. I was content with my family and I had many friends. Life was easy. I worked hard during the week, but I could call the weekends my own. I spent them relaxing with my wife and children—until that fateful moment.

That moment at Paqueta Island is the moment that I try to forget but cannot, the time that I must look at once again if I am to tell this story. My emotions do not want to revisit that day, but my intellect tells me I must.

It is Sunday in December, two days before Christmas. In Brazil, it is summer. I am with my family on Paqueta. Although I do not know it yet, it is the last day of my first life.

The city of Rio de Janeiro encircles one of the loveliest harbors in the world, in which is set the island of Paqueta, called by many people the island of love, and understandably so. From Rio, it takes about an hour by motor launch to this small but very, very beautiful island. It is a paradise of velvet lawns and tropical plants and flowering trees, which Brazilians take for granted. One can see tremendous trees with every inch of foliage covered with flamboyant flowers. Every tree is a different color. Sometimes a tourist will gasp at the breathless beauty, turn to a Brazilian, and ask, "What is that?"

And the Brazilian will answer, "What is what?"

The tourist will say, "That magnificent tree with all the red flowers. What kind is it?"

The Brazilian will answer, "Oh, that's a tree covered with red flowers."

Such beauty is taken for granted on Paqueta.

In Paqueta there is a law which some people say is too old to be written, so it was handed down by the gods. The law says that it is forbidden to work. Here one is expected to lie in hammocks and sip fruit juice. There is no output of energy. It is said that on Paqueta, even the birds walk. Within ten feet of our house on the beach, there are at least ten kinds of fruit growing, and there are wild orchids.

That weekend we have guests, and there is much laughter and gaiety. The rhythmic sounds of guitars set feet to dancing and voices singing. Such a happy and carefree time. My wife Lourdes is talking to friends. They laugh at a funny story. I see who has told the story—a good friend. I smile because only a few minutes before he told the same story to me.

I see my nine-year-old daughter Lourdinha getting more fruit punch with her friends. I think of how lovely she is—I rarely look at her without thinking this. She looks over at me and smiles.

I look at the sun. It is low in the sky. It is after five o'clock, I say to myself, and turn toward the water and call to my son, Jose ZeCarlos, and tell him it is time to get out of the water.

"Oh, Papa, let me dive one more time," he begs. "The others are still swimming."

It is still warm, so I do not argue. I say, "All right. One more dive and that is all."

I watch him as he runs across the beach, the water splashing on his strong, brown legs. He is thirteen years old. Soon he will be a man. He climbs up the rock with little effort. When he gets to the top, he pauses for a moment and waves to me. Then he stretches his arms into the air and, like a graceful bird, dives into the water.

I turn away and start to join the others. But suddenly I feel uneasy. I look back at the water. I wait for a moment for ZeCarlos to come up. I do not see him. Everybody is still laughing and having a good time. "Where is ZeCarlos?" I ask myself. Then I start walking toward the beach, and before I know it, I am running into the ocean and swimming to the waters that had swallowed my son. I call up to the other divers on the rocks and say, "Look down! Do you see my son?"

"Yes," one calls back and points toward a place in the water. I swim there. Taking a deep breath, I dive down into the darkness straight to my son and pull him into my arms.

I carry him out of the water and up on the beach. I see that his head is turned to the side in an unnatural way.

"ZeCarlos, are you all right?" I ask, already fearing what the answer will be.

"I can't move my arms and legs," he tells me.

"Try to raise your arms."

"I can't," he says. "I can't."

I suddenly feel dizzy and sick in my stomach. I want to

push back the hands on the clock—three minutes would be enough for me to call to him, "No, you cannot make one more dive. You come in now. Don't argue with me, my son. My ZeCarlos, do not argue with...."

"Try to move your legs, just a little bit. Try!"

"I can't, Papa. I can't."

I want to scream.

By this time, my wife is with us, and she is crying. A friend bends down next to me and says, "Raymundo, what's wrong?"

"His neck is broken," I say.

The last minute of my first life is ended; my second life begins.

I do not leave my son's side. I stay with him in the hospital; because I am a doctor, it is easy for me to arrange. Within hours the finest specialists in Brazil see my son. They tell me he is paralyzed from the neck down and that within two or three weeks he will die. I listen to them, but I refuse to believe it. I pray, "Dear God, don't let this be so. Help me find a way to make my son well." Then I make a bargain with the Lord. I tell Him if He will help me make ZeCarlos better, I will devote my life to making other people's children well. From the hospital, I call my secretary and tell her to close my office.

She asks me, "For how long?"

"Forever. I will not be back."

I call my brother and tell him I need him to help. He comes to the General Hospital, and we prepare to take ZeCarlos to my clinic.

The neurosurgeon says, "You can't do this."

I say, "Why not?"

"If you move him, he will die."

I tell him, "If he stays here, you say, he'll die in two or three weeks. Get out of my way."

He says, "I hope you realize that you take full responsibility."

I tell him, "I long ago took responsibility for my son."

From the General Hospital to my clinic is a half-hour drive, but this night it takes us three hours. My brother Julio drives the car slowly so that ZeCarlos is not bumped or moved in any way.

Once we are in my clinic, I am in command. I have them put my son in traction so his neck is straight and he cannot move. I have another bed brought into his room and have my wife bring clothes to the clinic, and I live in that room with my son. I prove the neurosurgeon at the General Hospital wrong. Three months later my son is still alive. The fracture has mended, but he is still paralyzed.

"What do I do now?" I ask myself. What good is it to keep him alive if he cannot be a person? I must find help for him. I know it is useless to look for such help in Brazil, because already the best doctors have seen him, and they have said that they can do nothing for him. During the War, when I was in the Army in Italy, I became aware that the United States medical people were more advanced than us in methods of therapy. So I decide to take my son to the United States. I am convinced that if I would ever find help for my son, it would be there.

From Rio de Janeiro to New York City is 5,500 miles. Today, by jet, the trip takes 9 hours, but in 1957 the propeller plane took 24 hours. Everything must be planned to the last detail. ZeCarlos is taken from the clinic to the airport in an ambulance. Using two seats in the airplane, we make a bed for him. Another ambulance will meet us at the airport in New York, and we will take him directly to the Institute of Physical Medicine and Rehabilitation, which is world famous for its advanced therapy for quadriplegics.

"Be brave, my son," I tell ZeCarlos. "Your mother and I are with you."

2

Disagreeable Objectives

Iɴ the airplane, my thoughts reel with invading images. Over and over I see my son dive into the water. Imagine, if you will, the terror that grips the swimmer once his neck is broken. He is beneath the water; in order to come to the top for a breath of air, he must be able to move his arms and legs, but because his neck is broken, he has no command over his limbs — he is completely helpless. He cannot call out for help; he can only hope that someone will see him and come to him before he drowns. What terror it must be. I see this in my nightmares.

I have high hopes about the Institute of Physical Medicine and Rehabilitation, but after only a few days I become very disturbed. I see many paraplegics and quadriplegics sitting in comfortable rooms watching television. Much of the therapy is nothing more than training these people to use special equipment.

Almost instinctively, I realize that the goal to train someone to be content with his inabilities is as bad as having no goal at all.

Does one need to be trained to be paralyzed? Does one need incredibly expensive hospitalization to make one what he already is? First as a father, then as a doctor, I see that there is something tragic in the idea of a happy, well-adjusted cripple. I am convinced there surely must be a better objective for human beings.

I am aware of the fact that historically nothing has been done for paralyzed people. They used to die early deaths from kidney infections from the inactivity of lying in bed. Surely during the last fifty years there have been improvements. In the 1950s, therapists proposed that it's better to be a useful cripple than a useless cripple. This idea has received much support since World War II, especially in the work of Dr. Rusk and Henry Viscardi and many others. But I'm not looking for my son to be a useful cripple. I want my son to be as noncrippled as he can be, and I talk to Dr. Rusk about this many times.

I say, "Dr. Rusk, with these methods, your staff is training my son to become a successful quadriplegic. I do not want him to become a successful quadriplegic. I want him to become a person. I want him to use his arms and legs. I want him to move around. I do not want him to sit all day and watch television."

Dr. Rusk is a very nice man. He listens to me very kindly and then says, "You want the impossible. You must adjust to realities. Your son is a quadriplegic, and he always will be."

"If we treat him like a quadriplegic, then I agree that that is the way he will stay. But that is not what I want. I want him to be made well."

"That is impossible," Dr. Rusk tells me many times.

I am sure he must think I'm crazy. I am sure he says to his staff, "Be nice to this man Veras. He's a little bit crazy but not dangerous. But watch him anyway."

For me and my wife, it is a very discouraging time.

You must understand that being a quadriplegic—not having command of one's arms and legs—is not twice as bad as being a paraplegic and not having the use of two limbs. It is a thousand times worse. When one has the use of either his arms or his legs, he has many ways to save his life in case of an emergency. If he has use of his arms, he is mobile. He can get into a wheelchair by himself if necessary. He can pick up something to protect himself. But the quadriplegic is immobile and completely helpless. He is at the mercy of other people and circumstances. He has no command over his present condition and no choice over his future. He is a head with a useless body. He is a brain that can only speak and hear. His world is limited to those persons and things that can be brought into his room. He must be fed and must be cleaned. There is no privacy for him. He is exposed to a thousand deaths.

I tell my wife that our pilgrimage must come to an end, that it is useless for us to stay at this place. I tell her that it would be best to return to Brazil, because I think that there, since their methods are more primitive and their personnel is not so well trained, perhaps they will get ZeCarlos to regain some feeling in his body. I say this for her benefit, but I do not believe this myself. When I am alone, I cry.

My wife pretends, too. She listens to me and tells me that she is sure that I am right, but in her heart, she knows that my words are only idle wishes. We prepare to leave the United States.

Only a few blocks from our hotel is St. Patrick's Cathedral. In mid-morning, my wife walks there and prays for our safe return to Brazil. It is a quiet hour. Most people in New York are either working or in a hurry to get from one place to another. Except for one man, the cathedral is empty. My wife walks to the altar and lights a candle. Then she kneels to pray. No sooner does she start than her words become tears. She tries to control her emotions, but she cannot. She cries aloud. Finally she is able to stop her sobbing, and she wipes the tears from her eyes and stands up to leave. When she reaches the front door, the man steps forward and says, "Excuse me. I don't mean to interfere, but I couldn't help but notice your crying. You must have terrible troubles. Is there anything I can do to help you?"

My wife does not know that people in New York are supposed to be unfriendly and uncaring. She starts talking and doesn't stop until she has told this stranger all about our son's condition.

When she is finished, the man tells her, "I have heard of a rehabilitation center in Philadelphia. I don't know its name, but I hear they do wonderful work with people like your son."

My wife is very excited when she comes back to the hotel. "There is a placc in Philadelphia where they can make ZeCarlos well. We must go there."

"How do you know this?" I ask.

"The man at the cathedral told me."

"What is the name of this place?"

"He isn't sure," she answers.

"He isn't sure about the name, and yet you tell me we must go to Philadelphia?" I say. "What kind of sense does that make?"

"Would you argue with an angel?" she replies.

"What angel?" I ask.

My wife looks straight at me and announces, "The man at the cathedral is an angel. I am sure."

Sometimes I do not understand myself. I am a reasonable man, a man of logic. Yet that afternoon I am on a train to Philadelphia because of nothing more than hearsay. And I do not believe for one minute that this man at the cathedral is an angel. If he was an angel, why did he not know the name of this place he told her about and why didn't he know the address?

3

The Search

As soon as I check into a hotel in Philadelphia, I begin my search for this place that my wife's angel tells her about. I ask people at the hotel if they have heard of this place. They are very kind but say they've never heard of it. A nice young man looks through the telephone book for me but cannot find the place I describe.

I go to the Red Cross. They say they will try to help me. I talk to the people at the Brazilian Consulate. They also say they will look. Everyone tells me to be patient—it's so easy to tell me that. ZeCarlos is not their son. While I wait, I call a detective agency and soon have an investigator on duty. Finally (I don't recall why I think of it), I call the Coffee Institutes of Brazil. In a couple of hours, they call me back and say, "The place you are looking for is the Rehabilitation Center at Philadelphia." They give me the telephone number, and I call.

The woman I speak to has trouble understanding my English. She asks what language I normally speak. I tell her Portuguese. She asks me to wait, and after a minute she comes back and asks if by any chance I speak Spanish. I tell her yes.

Colonel Antonio Flores comes to the phone. I tell my story to him in Spanish. He tells me that he is not sure if they can take ZeCarlos, but he invites me to come see the kind of work they are doing. I tell him I will get in a taxi this minute. I think he meant for me to come the next day, but he understands my urgency and is too courteous to tell me to wait.

I arrive at The Rehabilitation Center and meet Colonel Flores. I learn that he is the associate director. I like him immediately.

Tony Flores is both physically and emotionally a strong man. He was born in the United States of Spanish ancestry and speaks Spanish extraordinarily well. He has an unusual background. He was responsible for writing many of the Army field manuals on unarmed defense, and over one hundred of the pictures in those books are of him. He is a first-rate physical educator.

A strange thing about this man. He had once been a very hairy person, the kind that has a five o'clock shadow before noon. Then at Army Reserve camp one year, while taking a shower, he was struck by lightning, and within a few days all of his hair fell out. Now he has no eyebrows, no eyelashes, no body hair anywhere — not even in his nose. He used to put cigarette filters in his nose. He looks something like Winston Churchill — as bald as a baby, but very strong.

As I follow Colonel Flores around the Center, my hopes are raised because of the things I see. Here there are no paraplegics sitting watching television; instead they are involved in physical therapy to improve their functions. I also see that the quadriplegics are not left to vegetate. Therapists are working with them to try to revitalize sensation in their limbs. Within a few minutes I know that this is exactly the place I am looking for.

I ask Colonel Flores if I can bring ZeCarlos to this place as a patient. I remember that he said he would ask. We walk down a hallway, and he tells me to wait for a minute and then disappears into a room. He returns with a young man, whom he introduces as Glenn Doman, the director.

I shake this man's hand. I remember I think he is quite young to be the director. I recognize that he is a very strong man with much energy—very outgoing. He is friendly, but it is also obvious that he is busy. We speak for only a few minutes, and then he and Colonel Flores walk back into the room. When Colonel Flores comes back to me, he says, "You can bring your son here. It's arranged."

Then in my heart, I know my wife is right—the man at the cathedral is indeed an angel.

4

Sensuous Activities

My wife and I realize that ZeCarlos's therapy will require long-term patience and long-term plans. We decide that I will stay in Philadelphia with our son and watch over his progress. Lourdes will return to Brazil and to our daughter Lourdinha, who has been staying with friends.

Now our family is separated by 5,000 miles. It is a time of many hopes and prayers and much loneliness.

Every day I watch ZeCarlos's therapy at The Center. Never before have I seen such methods used. It quickly becomes obvious to me that I am watching great advances in medicine.

The therapists are very observant, and they utilize their observations to alter treatment. I see this many times — someone makes a mistake, and something good comes from it. It is the history of medicine.

For example: The life of a quadriplegic is in danger at all times. He can sit beside a radiator and burn holes in his legs without knowing it until he smells himself burning. Or he can sit on a fold in his underwear for half an hour and develop a bedsore on his buttocks so large that a soup bowl could be placed inside.

However, at The Center, the staff members began to suspect what very few people realize even today—that very few people with injured spinal cords have *completely* severed cords. The therapists at The Center suspect that very few cord-injured people are completely without sensation. It was very, very bright for them to suspect this. And quite advanced.

Most people do not realize that blind people are almost never completely blind and that deaf people are almost never completely deaf.

It is very important that I make this clear. Often blind people are blind because they are treated as if they were completely blind. People who have hearing problems become completely deaf because they are treated as if they were already deaf. And often partially paralyzed people become completely paralyzed because they are treated as if they were already paralyzed. Often the patient becomes what the therapist treats him to be. If this fact is used in a negative way, then it is sad. But if it is used in a positive way, then it is often very happy for the patient, because he becomes much better—sometimes completely well.

The majority of paraplegics are diagnosed and labeled without anyone's having actually looked at their spinal cords. Most of them have not had laminectomies. When the physician has performed a laminectomy, we often find on the medical charts a surgical note stating something like, "We opened the patient and prepared the surgical field, but it was grossly bloody, so we stopped." If the surgeons do proceed, we find a note stating, "Found that spinal cord was grossly intact." But no matter what the surgical note says, almost all of these patients are treated as if their spinal cords had been severed.

Today, Dr. Temple Fay is referred to as the dean of neurosurgeons and is respected as a genius. He made many great advances in the field of medicine. But in his lifetime he was very controversial because he was years ahead of his time. He was the first man to refrigerate the human body during surgery (a method widely used today in heart surgery), but he was denounced for attempting such a thing. For several years he was Chief of Neurosurgery at The Center, and his influence had much impact on the thinking of the staff members. Dr. Fay made them aware that only very rarely did cord-injured people have completely severed cords, and only very rarely were paralyzed people completely without sensation.

At The Center there are many cord-injured people. The staff had long suspected that since these patients were not completely without sensation, there might be some way to improve their sensation. One day, a happy accident occurs. A therapist is applying heat to a patient's foot, and she accidentally burns a blister on his toe. Because circulation is often poor in paralyzed limbs, there is always great danger of infection, so much attention is given to the healing of the burn.

Several days later, a nurse walks by the foot of the patient's bed and touches his toe. To her surprise, the patient says, "Ouch." This is much like touching a dead man and having him suddenly sit up. This patient was paralyzed from the waist down, but now he feels something. The nurse tells everyone, and soon the whole staff is standing at the foot of this patient's bed. Like children with a new toy, they take turns making the poor paralyzed man say, "Ouch."

They begin to wonder if they might be able to create the same thing in other patients. Obviously, they can't burn all their patients' toes, but what they do is ingeniously innovative. They assign one nurse, a tiny woman named Florence Sharpe (everyone calls her Sharpie), to cause burns by sandpapering. She takes a very, very fine piece of sandpaper and, using much alcohol to protect against infection, carefully sandpapers a patient's toe. She abrases the area until it weeps, removing only the outer layers of the skin, not going down so far that the area would bleed. Then she uses that tender area to develop sensation.

No one can settle on a title for Sharpie. Everyone today speaks in terms of sensory input and motor output—sensation and tactility. But in those days such terms were nonexistent. Some of us call her a sensationalist. And she is often introduced as the person in charge of sensual activity. It raises many eyebrows, which she enjoys greatly.

They begin this therapy on ZeCarlos, and sure enough, he, too, responds. It is too good for me to believe.

Two French physicians, John and Elizabeth Zuchmann, are fascinated with this method of developing sensation, so much so that they call their chief physician to come from France to see it. He is a very prominent French physician, also a count, very handsome and pompous. They bring him into my son's room for a demonstration. They blindfold ZeCarlos and then touch his toe. He responds, after which they do such things as pinch his toe and scratch it and ask him to identify what they are doing—which he does successfully. Then the Zuchmanns go into the hall to discuss this with the French physician. It's obvious they have vast respect for this man. They say to him, "Sir, what do you think?" And in all seriousness he answers, "Very simple. It's black magic." Then he leaves The Center and goes home to France.

It's hard to believe that such stupidity exists in the world. It embarrasses me to see men of my profession have so little curiosity. I did not formerly believe that there were many like this French doctor, but I have found to my great sorrow that there are many cast in his mold.

Although I am very happy with the work that the therapists do with ZeCarlos, I become disturbed. I have always been an active man. Every day I come from the hotel and watch the work that they do with my son. Having so little to do, I feel useless; my hands get nervous, and my mind becomes anxious to learn more.

I have an idea. I go to Colonel Flores and ask him, "Is it possible that I can become a student in this place?"

He tells me he will find out if it is possible.

5

Dr. Fay's Invention

COLONEL Flores must ask Glenn Doman about my becoming a student. For a month I have watched Glenn Doman, and I have grown more and more impressed with him. I have never seen a man with more energy. He never knows when it is time to go home—perhaps because his work is his home. His wife Hazel is truly a remarkable woman. She seems to understand this drive. She works by his side as a registered nurse.

In the beginning, I don't fully understand Glenn Doman's role in this extraordinary place. I know that he is director, and it is obvious to me that he is efficient and extremely bright. In time I will learn that he is more than bright—I will see his genius unfold. But for now I see him as a physical therapist and director of The Center. He is the man who has the power to say yes or no to my request to become a student.

Glenn Doman says yes. I am given a scholarship to be a student for one year. I soon learn that *student* is probably not the proper word for my newly acquired status. *Slave* would be a better title. But, I believe myself to be the luckiest slave in the world.

Now my days are full of work. The first month, I am assistant to a nurse. The second month, I am assistant to a physical therapist. Then for a month I am assistant to an occupational therapist, and so on. In twelve months I have twelve titles. I crawl with patients. I bathe patients. I try my best to do all that is asked of me, and because I appreciate the work they do with my son, I look for more work than I am told to do. And every day I learn something new. These people know more about the brain and brain injury than any people I have ever heard of. It is the most exciting place for me to be.

There is no time wasted. Even lunch time is utilized. Each day the staff meets at lunch so that Glenn Doman can ask questions, and we discuss patients' conditions and improvements. It is in these meetings that I begin to realize that it's not by coincidence that so many good therapists are working in the same place. I also begin to realize that Glenn Doman has a special talent for finding superior people to work with him, and he takes great joy in building their expertise. He gives more to them than he takes from them. If a nurse comes there as a pretty good nurse, he soon tells everyone that she is the best damned nurse in the world. It isn't so important that everyone else believes that she is the greatest thing since Florence Nightingale as long as the nurse herself starts to believe it. When she believes it, then that is what she becomes—the best damned nurse in the world. Or the best therapist, or whatever. Glenn Doman had, and still has, this talent of bringing out the best in the individual. If we could bottle that skill by the ounce, it would sell higher than Chanel No. 5.

The staff that Glenn has assembled is a composite of unique specialists and personalities. They have only one thing in common, and that is the urgency to improve the patient. I should make it clear that the patients at the Center are not given thirty minutes of therapy each day—they are on a regular eighteen-hour schedule with intense stimulation and physical activity. Staff members who don't share the common goal and aren't willing to expend long hours and develop tired muscles aren't staff members very long—not because they're fired but because they find eight-hour time clocks somewhere else.

Those who remain are bright, energetic individualists and idealists. At that time there was Robert Doman, M.D., a physiatrist (and Glenn's brother); Carl Delacato, an educator and psychologist; Hazel Doman, a registered nurse (and Glenn's wife); Eleanore Bordon, a physical therapist; Rosemary Boyle, chief nurse (who was both brilliant and a little crazy. Her statements alternated between the wildest kinds of nonsense and the most lucid insights). And, of course, there were Tony Flores and Sharpie. All were remarkable people.

In that year of 1957, the therapists at the Center were already making a name for themselves. Dr. Edward LeWinn of the Albert Einstein Medical Center was referring patients to this zealot group, and Dr. Eugene Spitz, a top pediatric neurosurgeon, was insisting that a preference should be given to children since their recuperative powers exceed those of adults and their life expectancy is longer.

With the attention they received, there was also, in the distance, a growing tide of professional jealousy and doubting Thomases. As much as there was a feeling that something new, perhaps revolutionary, was happening here, there was also an aura of controversy developing about this extraordinary work. I think it is fair to say that some of this controversy came from Dr. Temple Fay's association with the Center. His theories of brain development and its relationship to human function were still not understood by many. The world does not welcome new ideas.

It might be said that Glenn Doman is an invention of Dr. Fay's. It may be said that, at that time, he was both the best functional neurologist and the worst functional neurologist in the world, because he was the only functional neurologist.

I should also say that Glenn Doman paid Dr. Fay the greatest compliment that a student can pay his teacher—he took all that he had learned from his long association with Fay and built on that knowledge with his own genius. There was one basic difference between Doman and Fay, and that difference had divided them as a working team. Fay was a researcher. Doman is an applier. Fay saw his goals best served in the laboratory. Doman's goal was, and is, to affect the lives of people in positive ways. It was an irreconcilable difference.

In 1957, Glenn Doman was young and vigorous. He was also an idealist, convinced that right conquers wrong and that truth is triumphant. The most important thing to him was that his group was achieving remarkable results with stroke patients and brain-injured people.

I thank God that my son is at The Center.

I am overjoyed to become a part of this work.

And I am sure that the best is yet to come.

In those days I was an optimist.

6

Homesick

Although I am privileged during this year to learn so much and am overjoyed to see ZeCarlos progress, I grow more and more homesick for my wife and my daughter. I am homesick, too, for Brazil. I realize that we no longer have to remain in the United States for ZeCarlos's treatment. Now that I have the therapeutic methods in my head, I can take them home with us.

I tell Colonel Flores that I've decided to take ZeCarlos back to Rio. It's important to me that he be Brazilian. He speaks more English every day, and he's picking up American attitudes. There's nothing wrong with these attitudes for Americans, but I don't want my son to be a foreigner in his own land. I ask Colonel Flores if he will arrange a time for me to talk with Mr. Doman. He says he will.

During this year, I have grown to admire Mr. Doman, but I'm not sure that he knows my feelings, because we have talked so little. My English is like chicken noises, and he doesn't speak

21

Portuguese. At the staff meetings, I understand all that is said, but I don't talk much. It's much easier for me to hear English than to speak it. So I'm not sure what Mr. Doman thinks of me. For all I know, he may think my thoughts are as few as my words. I think if he has much respect for me, then he must have caught that from Colonel Flores, because the two of us have become close friends.

When the time for the meeting arrives, I am most anxious.

"Mr. Doman," I say, "when my son ZeCarlos had his accident, I think, 'Oh, my God, how can I live?' The doctors tell first that he will not live. They say this to me like they do me a favor. But my son does not die. I pray to the Lord that he will show the way to help my boy. I promise him that if he will do this, then I will spend the rest of my life making other kids like ZeCarlos well."

He listens and does not interrupt.

"With your permission," I continue, "I take ZeCarlos home to Brazil and do your therapy with him there. I also take your methods with me, and if you do not object, I will open a rehabilitation center in Rio."

"That's very kind of you, Dr. Veras," he says to me. "If it is your wish to open a center in Rio, you certainly have every right to do exactly that. But I hope that you will do this only because this is what you want, not out of gratitude to us."

"No, that is not the reason," I tell him. "I have an agreement with the Lord."

He smiles. "I learned a long time ago not to interfere with the Lord's legal matters. I will be most eager to hear of your work. And our best wishes go with you."

Then I presume even further with this man.

"When I begin my clinic," I say to him, "you must come to Brazil and see it for yourself."

"I would like nothing better," he answers.

"Then it is agreed," I say, extending my hand.

"It is agreed," he replies with a handshake.

No sooner does he say this than his secretary comes into the room and reminds him of another meeting. He shakes my hand and excuses himself while I keep trying to tell him of my undying gratitude. Poor man, he has to pull himself from my grasp, and he almost runs from the room. In later years, I learn that this man becomes very nervous when people thank him, and he will do almost anything to avoid extended good-byes.

I take my son home.

7

Centro de Reabilitacao NaSa da Gloria

Wʜᴇɴ we leave The Center, I don't think that Glenn Doman will be surprised if he never again hears from me. He had been given many idle promises before in his life, and he will be given many more later. But I know that my promise is not an idle wish. I will make it a reality.

I think that most North Americans have a very odd idea of what South Americans are like. They think we laze about all day with sombreros over our eyes and serapes draped across our shoulders, sleeping in the shade and mumbling about *mañana* should anyone wake us. I assure you, that view is as false as the one many Latin Americans have of the people in the United States—people who drive around in Cadillacs, consume enormous quantities of chocolate and Coca-Cola, and use their political leaders for target practice.

Most North Americans also have the misconception that all South American countries are alike. This, too, is untrue.

Brazil is totally unlike the other South American countries.

Others are Spanish in origin and have imported the Spanish language and culture. The Spanish have a rather sad and haughty culture. There are great feelings of tragedy in the Spanish makeup. Brazilians, on the other hand, are Portuguese in origin. They're happy, independent, freedom-loving people. Far from being sad and haughty, they're very light and happy people. They have a great sense of love and charity. And Brazil, unlike the other nations of South America, is run by the middle class.

Everything about Rio is breathtakingly beautiful, from the black-and-white mosaic sidewalks to the superb ocean beaches of Copacabana and Ipanema and Botofogo and the downtown. And only three blocks away, mountains rise 3,000 feet above the beaches.

If you stand in the middle of Rio, you're one and a half blocks from the ocean and one and a half blocks from the mountains. The good Lord truly went mad when he built Rio, which gives rise to a typical Brazilian story. The Brazilians say that when God built the world, in every country He built one natural disaster and one thing of great beauty. When He built Brazil, He lavished beauty everywhere, but He made no natural disaster. Brazil has no earthquakes, no tidal waves, no typhoons, no cyclones. So when God finished, His helpers turned to Him and said, "Sir, you have made this beautiful country, but you have made no natural disasters. Why is that?"

And God turned to them and answered, "Wait till you see the people I put there."

The most important thing must come first, I believe. My first responsibility is not to all people who need help. It is to my son. I do therapy with him every day and immediately enroll him in a regular school. I would never, never, never send him to a school for cripples. It is most important that I make the reader understand that I want my son to become a normal person. I do not want him to live in a cripple's world with a cripple's attitudes. I arrange for him to go to school for three hours on weekdays and six hours on Saturdays. I take him to school every day. And I see him become more normal.

This is so important, and few people really understand it. If we segregate people from normal people because they are hurt or because they are unusual, then they become stranger and stranger. If we want our children to be like normal children, then we must make a normal environment for them. Children learn to be normal. I believe this. I know this.

Within a month, I have another patient. Then another. I move furniture out of some of the rooms in my house, and they become therapy rooms. I soon need workers. I need someone who is physically strong. A prize-fighter becomes my first therapist. In a few weeks, I hire a Russian nurse. I now have patients, and I have a staff. I decide it is time to have a dedication. I send Glenn Doman an airline ticket with a letter telling him that I have kept my promise and that I look forward to seeing him as we discussed. I think he's very surprised — so much so that he agrees to come to my country for the dedication.

In what had been my living room, the Great Bishop Dom Brazil, Glenn Doman and his wife, a dozen patients and their families, and my family assemble. Glenn Doman and the Bishop cut a ribbon. The ribbon is composed of red, white, and blue for the United States and green and yellow for Brazil.

And that begins our association and our visits to each other. Since 1958 I've been to the United States more times than I can count, and Glenn has been to Brazil as often.

8

"Raymundo, as you know..."

MANY nice things happen while Glenn Doman visits with me. We immediately understand each other. It makes no difference whether I speak in Portuguese or he speaks in English — we know immediately not only what the other says but what he thinks. We become like brothers.

I think this trip is also very good for Glenn because it is the first opportunity he has had in a long time to rest, to stop for a few minutes and examine his thoughts.

One afternoon we are lying in hammocks, and Glenn says, "Raymundo, as you know..."

In years to come I learn that when Glenn says, "Raymundo, as you know," it is not the beginning of a sentence; it is the start of a discussion that often lasts far into the night.

"Raymundo, as you know, " he says, "classical treatment has never worked for the brain-injured child. In fact, it hasn't worked so consistently that no one expects it to. In most medical circles, making a brain-injured child well is considered not only an impossible goal but an immoral one also. The reason why classical treatment has never worked on brain-injured children is because it is unscientific, it is unmedical, it is irrational, and if all of those things are not good enough arguments against it, then add to them our original observation, the fact that it just doesn't work."

I nod my head and say, "Yes."

"There are two ways to look at a severely brain-injured child," he continues. "One. He has something wrong with his eyes because he doesn't see right. He has something wrong with his ears because he doesn't hear right. He has something wrong with his mouth because he doesn't talk right. He has something wrong with his throat because he doesn't swallow right. He has something wrong with his chest because he doesn't breathe right. And he can't move, so he must have something wrong with his left shoulder, his right elbow, left wrist, right hand, left knee, right ankle. And he is in diapers, so he must have something wrong with his bowels and his bladder.

"If a brain-injured child is seen in this way, then it would be important to get him an eye doctor, an ear doctor, a chest doctor, a left-shoulder doctor, a right-ankle doctor, and a bowel-and-bladder doctor."

I laugh.

"If this appears ridiculous, I can only say that if you show me a severely brain-injured child, I'll show you a kid who has been to an eye doctor, mouth doctor, chest doctor, and bowel-and-bladder doctor, etc.

"Two. You can look at the severely brain-injured child as a child who, because of an injury to his brain, has a seeing, hearing, feeling, talking, walking, running problem."

"That's true," I say.

"Recently I have become very disturbed about our work at The Center," he says.

"How's this?" I ask.

"I am disturbed for good reasons, thank God, instead of

bad ones. We've made a lot of progress in our methods of therapy. You know we're a thousand light-years ahead of everyone else, but I think we still have a lot more to learn. In the last year, I cannot help but notice, the children we have on these programs have progressed much faster than the adults have."

"That's good," I say.

"Well, it is and it isn't," he replies. "It is if I want the children to get well faster. But if this means that children automatically get better faster than adults because they are children, then I have to stop and ask myself why are we spending so much time with adults?"

"What do you mean?"

"I mean, at the present time, we have twenty children at The Center and twenty adults. Now, if children respond better to the therapy than adults, how can I justify having the adults? Why not have forty children patients?"

"That's a good question," I tell him.

"Yes, it is," he said. "And it is one that I must answer. It is a moral question — and moral questions are more difficult than medical questions."

I see him sit and think for a few minutes.

"There is another thing that concerns me," he said. "Today we have about twenty staff members to take care of forty patients. That's very expensive for the patient's family, and it requires all of the time of these staff members to take care of the patients."

He sits upright and looks at me. "Dr. Veras," he says, "have I told you about my Saturday clinic?"

I shake my head no.

"Eugene Spitz, the neurosurgeon, keeps sending us patients, brain-injured children. We don't have room for them as patients. So some time ago I set up a Saturday clinic. We see the children and tell the parents how to do the therapy, and the parents take their children home and do a program of therapy in the home."

"Can parents do this?" I ask.

"Extremely well. Some of them are getting amazing results. And best of all, they can devote more hours to doing the program than it's possible to get from even the best staff."

"Do parents understand what they do?"

"Of course," he answers. "I explain it very carefully to them. I'll tell you the truth, they make the best damned therapists for their own kids that I've ever seen. They don't have to become experts on all brain-injured kids, only their own. These people are all very bright, and they catch on very quickly."

"I see," I say, nodding my head. "You work only with educated parents."

"Oh, my God, no," he says. "One family are dirt farmers from western Pennsylvania."

"And they are therapists?" I ask.

"Yessir."

"That's interesting," I admit.

"But that's only part of it," he says. "I sometimes see five or six kids on Saturday."

"That's good."

"It's better than good, because those are six kids who would not be getting treatment any other way. In a month, I sometimes see as many as twenty new kids and give their parents programs.

"The parents take the kids home, do the programs for a couple of months, and then I see the kids again. Don't you understand what that means?" he asks and then continues without waiting for an answer. "That means that on one day a week, one staff member is recommending therapy for more patients than twenty staff members can take care of working seven days a week. Using the parents as therapists is like having an army of paramedicals at our command."

"Very smart thinking," I tell him.

"Yes, it is," he naturally agrees. "But that poses another

problem for me. How can I justify having twenty staff members working full time to take care of only forty patients? If these twenty staff members, instead, were only evaluating kids and instructing the parents to do the work, why, we might be able to help hundreds of hurt kids instead of only forty."

"Do you think this is possible?" I inquire.

"I think maybe it is," he says.

As I remember, we lie back in our hammocks and fall asleep. But the dream that this man has does not drown in our dreams — it waits for the time when Glenn Doman will bring it to reality.

It doesn't have long to wait.

9

The Promise Bears Fruit

It does not take me long to realize that I'm losing my house. The therapy equipment takes more space than the rooms allotted for it. I must get a building before I lose my kitchen and my bedroom — and maybe even my wife.

I rent a building in Botofogo. On the first floor I arrange space for adult patients. The second floor is for children.

I soon understand Glenn's problem better and better. It's not easy to have the right number of therapists for the number of patients. I also learn that brain injury does not recognize whether a family can afford therapy. When I review the contract that I made with the Lord, I find there is no clause that says I will make only rich patients well, so I can't turn away those who cannot afford our work. My business friends ask me, "What's happened to you? Have you lost your mind?" I say, "Maybe."

As the number of patients and staff members grows, I see my bank account reduce. I will get used to this condition. The Lord makes a hard bargain.

I am sure that those must have been hard times, but in my memory those first two years pass before me as in a night's dream.

During this time, Glenn Doman and I exchange many letters. He tells me of the new things they are doing at the Center. And I tell him of our progress. Then in 1962, he writes me and says, "You must come to Philadelphia, because we have made more changes than could be described in a letter. You must see these things with your own eyes to believe them."

When I arrive in Philadelphia in July 1962, it does not take me long to realize that Glenn was right. There are so many changes, that, indeed, I have to see them to believe. The changes begin at the entrance. No longer does the sign say The Rehabilitation Center at Philadelphia. A new sign reads THE INSTITUTES FOR THE ACHIEVEMENT OF HUMAN POTENTIAL.

I soon learn that there are no more in-patients. Glenn had brought into reality exactly what he had mentioned that summer's day in Rio. Now he and the staff evaluate the children and train the parents to do their therapy. A revolutionary idea becomes a revolutionary reality.

During the first day I see the clinic in action and am impressed with its efficiency. I learn that Glenn Doman is having a love affair. Not with another woman — he has fallen in love with parents. This is amazing indeed. The medical world has a tradition that the doctor and the parents are enemies, or at least divided by attitudes. I hear professionals say that parents are stupid; you cannot believe a word they say.

But now I hear Glenn say, "These people are absolutely great! Look how bright they are. They do everything we tell them to do for their children and then more. They are the best therapists in the world for their own kids."

This may well be the most revolutionary idea Glenn has ever had. But revolutionary or not, in years to come I see that he is right. Because he believes the parents are bright, he speaks to them and explains the work of The Institutes to them. He answers their questions. He gives them information not only about their own child's condition but about brain injury in general. He is convinced that the better informed the parents are, the better therapists they will become.

By this time, I see that Glenn explains these new theories well to parents. I also see that because of this love affair he has with them, he has found his favorite audience. In years to come, I will hear him teach the parents many times. I will never grow tired of hearing his words. He makes it so clear.

A special note to parents of mongoloids: It is extremely important that you read this section carefully. If you understand all that is said, it will be easier for you to understand what I will tell you later about mongoloids.

I would like to set this scene for the reader. We are in the auditorium. It is kept cold on purpose so that everyone will be alert and wide awake. The audience is composed of twenty-five to thirty sets of parents. Glenn walks into the room and speaks.

"The Institutes does not agree with everybody in the world about brain-damaged children. Our disagreement begins with the diagnosis—begins even before that, in definition," Glenn explains, "then extends to diagnosis, classification, method, technique, and ends up in objectives.

"We place the children we see in three categories:
Deficient brain
Psychotic brain
And injured brain.

"Deficient brain—any child who at the moment of conception the good Lord did not intend to have a normal brain. Not at birth, not just before birth, not two weeks after, not one day after, but at the moment of conception.

"To our knowledge," he says, "nothing can be done for these children. Happily, we believe that these children are *extremely rare*.

"Psychotic brain—any child whose behavior is wildly different from other children his own age but whose brain appears to be physically normal.

"These are lovely children," he tells us, "but we can do nothing for them. Happily, they are also *extremely rare*.

"Injured brain—any child who at the moment of conception the good Lord intended to have a perfectly good brain. Later, the brain is injured in some way—incompatible Rh factor in the parents, mother had German measles during the first three months of pregnancy, lack of oxygen during prenatal term, etc.

"The staff at The Institutes knows about a hundred ways a child can suffer brain injury, and there are probably a thousand; premature delivery is most common in the brain-injured children we see."

He mentions many other factors that may produce a brain injury: overmature prenatal period, protracted labor (eighteen hours or more), delayed birth (perhaps due to the mother's late arrival at the hospital), induced labor, obstetrical difficulties, bumps on the head, drowning and revival, high fever due to measles or other upset, and cardiac or respiratory failure during simple surgery.

"There are approximately 100 billion cells in every child's head," Glenn says. "At least 10 billion of these are neurons, or nerve cells, capable of functioning as operating units of the brain. Ten billion is a difficult number to associate with reality even for an American taxpayer. To try to give some reality to this number, it's helpful to know that if your child had been born before Christ and used a brand-new brain cell every 10 seconds, 60 seconds a minute, 60 minutes an hour, 24 hours a day, 365 days a year, and if that child were still alive today, he would have more than 3 billion neurons that he hadn't yet used.

"Brain injury is the state that exists when one or more of these brain cells is dead.

"If it occurs to you that it would be difficult to imagine a human being having 10 billion neurons in the brain without a single one of them being dead, and that if such is indeed the case then in fact everyone is to some degree brain-injured. One would be hard put to refute that argument. There is a good deal of research to support the view that everyone has millions of dead brain cells, and recent research indicates strongly that some brain cells are destroyed every time a human being takes a single drink of beer, wine, or whiskey. This becomes even more believable when he learns that the researchers themselves stopped drinking during this particular study.

"The question then becomes not who is brain-injured and who is not, but rather *how* brain-injured each of us is.

"It's obvious that brain injury is a continuum, which ranges from so little that one appears to be completely well, to so much that the person so injured is dead.

"The larger the number of brain areas that contain dead cells, the greater the number of functions (such as walking, talking, reading, writing, hearing, understanding, feeling, etc.) involved. The larger the number of dead cells in any single brain area, the more severe will be the problem of walking, talking, reading, etc.

"Brain injury can occur at any time from the instant of conception onward, and the children seen at The Institutes for the Achievement of Human Potential in Philadelphia have sustained their injuries ten minutes after the instant of conception, ten hours, ten days, ten weeks, ten months, or ten years after that instant of conception.

"Not only is it possible for brain injury to occur prior to birth, but it is a fact that the vast majority of the brain-injured children seen at The Institutes have sustained their brain injuries prior to or during birth. A sampling indicated that less than ten percent of the children were hurt after birth. Less than two percent of the children seen at The Institutes are the product of postnatal external trauma such as automobile accidents.

"Many of the children we see have previously been labeled as cerebral palsied, mentally retarded, athetoid, autistic, 'slow learners,' and a host of other names. To say that these children have been *diagnosed* as having cerebral palsy or mental retardation would be both improper and unscientific, because neither of these are proper medical diagnoses. These are symptoms of a neurological dysfunction, not the cause. To say that a child has mental retardation would be like saying that he has a fever. No one believes that a fever is a disease, but because the terms *mental retardation* and *cerebral palsy* have been so sloppily used and misused, many people mistakenly think that these are diseases. Even within the medical establishment, where people should know better, these terms are used, misused, and abused. It is both confusing and embarrassing.

"Some of the children come here completely paralyzed, functionally blind, functionally deaf, or completely insensate," Glenn says. "On the other hand, we see a number of children from special education classes, and some from regular classrooms, who have learning problems. We see children from Pennsylvania, Iowa, Italy, and Argentina. One thing is clear — brain injury recognizes neither state nor national boundary; has no regard for class distinction; and has absolutely no respect for age.

"The brain, that most important organ, distinguishes man from other animals. The function of the brain," Glenn states, "is to relate its owner to his environment.

"A child grows from a microscopic one-cell organism at a fantastic rate of speed. At the moment of conception there is an explosion into growth. In twelve days the fetus has a brain and spinal column; in twenty-four days it has a beating heart; in nine months it has a weight of seven pounds. However, every day the rate of growth is less than the day before. Between the ages of seven and eight, a child's brain will grow almost the same amount it will between the ages of eight and eighty.

"In the first six years of life, a child learns more, fact for fact, than he will learn in the rest of his life.

"The brain," Glenn continues, "is a superb computer. It has a large advantage over its electronic copies — the more that's put in the human brain, the more it will hold; the more it is used, the better it works. As a computer, the brain must be programmed, and information must be fed into it. Everything goes into permanent storage in the brain of a three-year-old; he is being programmed.

"Due to the function of his brain, Man is set apart from other animals. Only Man stands up and walks in a cross pattern. Only Man talks in abstract symbolic language (the good Lord gave Man a superb brain for practical language; Man invented such languages as French, German, English, etc.) Only Man sees in such a way that he can read that language. Only Man hears in such a way that he can understand that language when it is spoken. Only Man can oppose his thumb to his forefinger and thereby write that language. Only Man can feel an object and know what it is without smelling, seeing, or tasting it.

"In other words, there are six functions that characterize Man — walking, talking, writing, reading, hearing, and feeling.

"It is the lack of one or all of these six functions that brings a child to The Institutes for the Achievement of Human Potential, and it is the presence of these six functions that graduates him from there.

"The function of the brain is to relate its owner to his environment," Glenn repeats. "The degree of efficiency with which that brain relates its owner to his environment is that child's degree of neurological organization.

"The world has looked on brain development or growth as a static and irrevocable fact. But this simply is not true. Brain development is a dynamic and ever-changing process — it can be stopped, it can be slowed, and, most significantly, it can be speeded up. We do the latter every day.

"In normal development, children go through four stages of mobility development. At birth the child moves his arms and legs. At two to three months he can move his arms in such a manner that he can move his whole body — he crawls. By seven to eight months he lifts his torso off the floor and moves on hands and knees — he creeps. Between nine months and a year he stands up and walks.

"We find that brain-injured children, no matter what age, cannot do one or all of these four things. They cannot move their arms and legs, or they cannot crawl properly, or they cannot creep properly, or they cannot walk properly. All of these things we expect in the development of a one-year-old, but a brain-injured child has not mastered at least one of them, sometimes two of them, sometimes three, and some can do none of them. Once brain-injured children can do these four things, they get better.

"Each of these four functions is controlled by the brain," Glenn says, "and each is necessary to neurological development. The brain is developed in four stages: the medulla and spinal cord, the pons, the midbrain, and the cortex.

"The medulla and spinal cord are developed at birth. They control the child's birth cry, light reflex, startle reflex, grasp reflex (the child can take hold of an object but cannot willingly let it go), Babinski reflex, and movement of arms and legs in a swimming motion. Now, not only do the medulla and spinal cord control the arms and legs in the aquatic motion, but this particular movement in turn activates more brain cells.

"The pons develops in the average child at approximately two and a half months. It controls outline perception, vital crying to threats of life, vital release (not only can the child grip an object, but now he can willingly let it go), vital response to threatening sounds, and perception of vital sensations such as extremes of hot and cold. The pons also controls crawling. At this time the child becomes mobile; he now begins to crawl on his stomach, combat-fashion, across the crib. At first he crawls homolaterally (left leg moving forward with the left arm, right leg moving forward with the right arm). Soon he develops a cross pattern (right leg moving forward with the left arm and vice versa). The cross pattern is an essential development, for later he will creep on hands and knees alternately. And eventually he will walk and run in a cross pattern (left arm moving forward as a counterbalance with the right leg, while the right arm co-ordinates with the left leg). When a child crawls in a cross pattern, he activates cells in the pons area.

"The midbrain develops when the child is about seven months old. It controls the creation of meaningful sounds, prehensile grasp (children at this age pick up objects as if their hands were encased in mittens), appreciation of detail within a configuration (at first a baby can see only the silhouette of his mother's face; now he begins to see her eyes, nose, and mouth), and appreciation of gnostic sensations (ability to distinguish more subtle differences of temperature). The midbrain also controls creeping on hands and knees—left hand forward as right knee moves forward, right hand co-ordinating with left knee in a good cross pattern. When a child creeps in a cross pattern, he activates cells in the midbrain.

"The cortex develops when the child is approximately twelve months. Then the child begins to use words spontaneously and meaningfully. He begins understanding spoken words. His eyes begin to converge, resulting in simple depth perception. He begins to understand the third dimension in objects that appear flat (such as a coin). The cortex controls cortical opposition (the use of the thumb and index finger to pick up objects) and walking in a cross pattern (left foot forward with right hand, right foot coordinating with left hand). When a child walks in a cross pattern, he activates more cells in the cortex."

If the reader has had the opportunity to see brain-injured children progress from the crawling stage to the creeping stage, he will not doubt what Glenn Doman has said is true. For the brain-injured child, the natural plan of development becomes a vicious circle. If the brain is injured in the medulla, the child moves his legs and arms poorly if at all. And if he does not move his legs and arms, more brain cells are not activated.

"Brain injury is in the brain," Glenn stresses. "We know dead cells are dead and cannot be revitalized. But in most brain-injured children there are enough additional cells to be activated. The brain, as a computer, must be programmed. If the child is unable to program movement of arms and legs, then it must be done for him. What goes into the brain," says Glenn, "must come out. Once the pattern of crawling is etched into the brain, the child will crawl. When he crawls, he activates cells in the pons area of the brain, and he starts doing the things other children can do, which are controlled by the pons.

"Today we know of seven nonsurgical and six surgical ways to treat injured brains," he says. "There are probably hundreds more. We're still looking.

"To give one example of surgical treatment: Over thirty-five thousand children are alive today due to one surgical method alone, the V-J shunt developed by Dr. Eugene Spitz to relieve hydrocephalic children with 'water on the brain.' Because of injuries, the cerebrospinal fluid that is constantly manufactured in the brain is not reabsorbed in the normal manner in these youngsters, and it builds up inside the skull, causing enlargement of the head and extreme pressure, which damages the brain. Once the V-J shunt is surgically in place, the excess cerebrospinal fluid drains through a tube via a special valve into the jugular vein. These children can now live normal lives.

"However, most of the children who come to the Institutes are treated by nonsurgical means, through specific ways of programming the brain through physical stimuli. This programming, they have found must be done with 'frequency, intensity, and duration' to increase the flow of information to the brain.

"The brain-injured child has barriers to the reception of sight and sound. These barriers must be broken. The child's environment must be tailored to his needs. The input of sensory impulses must be increased for the brain-injured child.

"To the brain-injured child," Glenn warns, "time is not a friend; it is an enemy. It's an impartial foe to every brain-injured kid alive. Any day a brain-injured kid isn't better, he is worse, because he's one day older and the other kid is one day better.

"Is there a mother of a hurt child," he asks, "who hasn't

thought of that over and over and over? Every day a brain-injured kid is not better, he is worse because he is a day older and every well kid is a day better.

"When we prescribe programs of intensified crawling and creeping for our patients, many of them achieve noticeable improvement. For children who are not able to either crawl or creep, our team has designed a method of moving the child's arms, legs, and head in a crawling motion known as *patterning*.

"A surgical team at an operating table," Glenn says, "during open brain surgery must have four qualities: (a) every member of the team has to be highly skilled at what he's doing; (b) they have to work skillfully together; (c) it's very hard physical labor; (d) they're working with that child's brain to save his life. This is open brain surgery.

"A patterning team has the same qualities: (a) every member of the team has to be highly skilled at what he's doing; (b) they have to work skillfully together; (c) it's very hard physical labor; (d) they're working with that child's brain to save his life. They are doing closed brain surgery.

"Patterning places precise information in the brain, informing the brain how it feels to crawl," Glenn states. "Once this information is utilized by the brain, the child can crawl on his own. These are in no sense physical exercises for the child; they are organized information inputs to improve brain function.

"We have seen hundreds of brain-injured children who, after they became able to crawl and creep properly, were able to stand up and walk on their own.

"Some of the programs seem impossible," Glenn warns, "and in lesser hands than a mother's, they *would* be impossible. Yet we rarely hear a mother complain, and often we find that mothers do more than we suggest. They want their children well.

"We have found mothers to be the best teachers and

therapists for their own children because they intuitively administer the proper portions of love and discipline and provide the security of a home environment.

"In a world that has long believed that brain function cannot be altered or improved, it is not surprising that some of our methods are questioned," Glenn says. "The questions should be asked, and they should be answered. Some of the best answers, of course, are our children. It is not surprising that we have failures, but what is surprising is that with increased regularity our children are getting better. What is even more significant, our successes are often children who have previously been diagnosed as 'incurable' or 'hopeless.'

"The Institutes is often regarded as the last resort. It's a rare family that brings a child to us without first having been to at least three other clinics or institutions. Many have been all over the world.

"So we set a goal for every child in our program—to enroll him eventually in a regular class with children his own age. Anything less than this, no matter how the child has been improved, the staff regards as a failure, The Institutes' failure. We achieve our goal with a significant number of children who had been declared hopeless.

"Our success comes from what we have learned and the enormous dedication of parents. Our failures stem from what we have yet to learn.

"Today," Glenn says, "we are still not satisfied with the progress we have achieved. If anything, our appetites for learning more about brain-injured children have intensified and our aggressiveness toward new goals has accelerated.

"Without knowing it, the brain-injured children and their parents have performed a great service for all the children of the world. Through them, we have learned successful ways to increase the ability of not only brain-injured children, but, indeed, of all children.

"If these methods of accelerating childhood development and brain growth are made available to healthy children, their potential for learning staggers the imagination."

Glenn has now brought all the information together. Never once during his orientations does he speak down to his audience. Some of the people there have no college or even high school education. Some parents are college graduates, some have master's degrees, and a few even have doctorates. It makes no difference. Glenn prefers to view them all as intelligent human beings. He treats them as equals.

This day, in the auditorium, I learn even more from this man.

In my heart I hope that someday I will find a way to repay him. But I wish that someday I might contribute more to his work. I do not know if this is possible, but I pray it will be so.

10

"My Poor Fool"

I become very excited about the changes I see in Philadelphia. In the month that I stay there, I learn much and get many new ideas. I see what Glenn means about children, and I become anxious to return to Rio so that I can tell my staff of these advances.

When I arrive in Rio, I call my staff together and tell them that from this time on we will take no more adult patients and that we will teach the parents to be therapists. I expect that my staff will catch my enthusiasm, but to my surprise they do not. They look at me as if I've gone a little crazy. It disturbs me that they don't understand. I tell myself that they will in time.

I go home, and that night I tell my wife about all the wonderful things that we are going to do. I think my wife will be enthusiastic, but when I finish she slowly shakes her head and says, "My husband, I feel very sorry for you. You've caught the Glenn Doman disease. If you do all of these things, you will have no life of your own. Don't you see that you are now spending more and more time with the therapy? I only see you late at night, and then you're so tired that we don't even talk. Our friends ask me, 'What's happened to Raymundo since he opened this clinic?' 'He has changed.' 'We do not know him.' I beg you, think of these things before it's too late."

"You don't understand," I tell her. "I will make these changes, build a good staff, and then become only an administrator. In about a year I'll be going to work at nine and coming home early in the afternoon just like a banker—you'll see."

My wife looks at me, tears come to her eyes, and she says, "My poor fool."

Perhaps my wife is right. Perhaps I am nothing but a poor fool. I don't know about that. All I know is that there are so many brain-injured children and their parents are desperate for help.

Barbacena is seven hours by bus. Before the end of 1961, I open another clinic there because parents in that city come and beg me to show them the therapy. I learn to sleep on the bus so I don't lose a workday. Now I travel back and forth. I spend twelve days in Rio and then two days in Barbacena.

The second clinic complicates my life, but I can't say no.

11

I Am Trapped

I always look forward to my visits to The Institutes. In the beginning, I think, "So much is happening and there are so many changes." I tell myself that in time everything will settle down. I watch Glenn work eighteen to twenty hours a day, and I see no harm in this. Perhaps that's my reaction because I am doing the same, and I think that young men are supposed to work — it's good for their souls. I keep telling myself that there are years of rest waiting for us in the not-too-distant future. It's a time of great energy and great naïveté. We have a feeling that fate has selected us and is leading us in the right direction.

It really isn't that simple. We aren't blindly following anything. We're working day and night, and we're paying dearly for whatever insights we gain. Glenn's mind seems always to be churning at ten thousand rpm. I don't think I've ever met anyone in my life who is more curious than he is about anything and everything. I think Glenn Doman is like a hyperactive three-year-old in a man's body and with a man's thoughts. He is constantly saying, "What is that? Why is that?" Answers to his questions only seem to give him fuel for more questions.

And then there is what I call the Doman build-up. It is a fearful and wondrous thing to behold. Because he feels that his work is so important and that the right people to help can make the difference between success and failure, he is extremely careful how he presents ideas to people.

I soon learn that it's very difficult to say no to Glenn. It's obvious why *I* find this almost impossible, because I am so grateful for what he has done for my son. But I'm not the only one who has this problem. I've seen many people come into Glenn's office to explain why they cannot do a certain thing, and before they leave they're telling him how simple a task this will be. Sometimes they've also volunteered to do two or three other jobs that have "just happened" to be mentioned in the conversation.

Very little "just happens." Those little ideas and spontaneous thoughts don't pop out of nowhere. They most often are plans that Glenn has been working out in his head, sometimes for months. And that person who "just happens by" hasn't really just happened by. Sometimes it has taken weeks or even months for Glenn to get the *right* person in the *right* room at the *right* time to hear the birth of the *right* idea to which that person can contribute the *right* skills.

In later years, after I have seen this many times, I have to laugh when someone walks out of his office and says, "You know, Glenn's really a nice guy, but he's a real chowderhead. Boy, is he lucky that I happened along. He never would have gotten this project going if it weren't for me."

Since I've watched this over and over and know how it works, I know how he sets his trap so the willing volunteers will help the "chowderhead" get things done. I am no exception. I am not immune to his enthusiasm and his dreams. Even when I realize that I am part of a plan, even when I can see that one of his conversations is a build-up to ask something of me, I cannot turn away or leave the room because I become too interested in finding out how he is going to build to his final question. I have often been tempted to stop him at the beginning of one of these persuasive orations and say, "The answer is yes to whatever you are going to ask me. Now convince me that my decision is right." I think of this answer in airplanes and on trains when there is plenty of time to figure out quick retorts, but when I am in the same room with him, I could never be so brash. Instead, I listen to him and watch myself being trapped neatly in his snare.

In the last months of 1962 or the early months of 1963 I arrive in Philadelphia, and Glenn meets me at the airport. In five minutes we bring ourselves up to date on each other's activities and briefly outline to each other the things of utmost importance to be accomplished during my stay. This is done very quickly because we do not waste words. Glenn will say, "Raymundo, what is the worst thing that has happened to you since we last talked?" I tell him. And then he will say, "And what is the best thing that has happened?" I answer him. Then I ask him the same questions. In minutes we know the best and the worst and we never ask about the in-betweens. It's not that we don't care; it's just that there isn't time.

When we get to The Institutes, instead of going down to the clinic or to Glenn's office as we usually do, Glenn takes me into the Board of Directors room and asks that lunch be brought to us. The board room is a room of great beauty, with mahogany-paneled walls and a huge table surrounded by twenty leather-upholstered chairs. We sit down to eat, and I notice an addition to the room. One wall is almost completely covered with a colorful map of the world. I have never seen a map this large before. Once in a movie I saw a map as big in what was supposed to have been Eisenhower's war room at the time of the invasion of Normandy.

I mention to Glenn how beautiful I think the addition is and in jest ask him if he intends to start a war.

He smiles and answers, "No. Not this year. Maybe next year."

We laugh.

I'm seated so that every time I look up I cannot help but see the map. As usual we discuss the progress of the kids. Then Glenn leans back in his chair, strikes a reflective pose, and says, "Raymundo, as you know..."

That should have been my clue. I am being set up, and here I am with that eager-as-a-lamb expression on my face.

"Raymundo, as you know, for a long time we have had the experience of seeing kids in our country who have very bad reading problems. I don't mean only slow readers; I mean kids who can't tell *dog* from *hippopotamus* or *cat* from *poison*. They have hardcore reading problems. These kids greatly interested Dr. Fay, and they interested us. We would examine these kids very carefully to see if we could find out what they had in common other than the reading problem. They had different backgrounds, different parents, came from different cities, had been given all kinds of teaching approaches to reading, but they couldn't learn. At the same time, many of these kids, by ear and by mouth, were smart as hell. They could understand all kinds of words and could carry on adult conversations. In other words, it was obvious that they weren't stupid. Many of them were very bright kids—they just couldn't learn to read."

I nod my head. I've heard most of this before, but a refresher course is always good for the student. And I realize that Glenn is not telling me this to pass the time, because I know full well that there are at least twenty people waiting to see him.

He leans forward. "We found that these kids had only two things in common. One—they couldn't read. Two—they couldn't creep correctly. When we had these kids creep for periods of time every day, their reading improved. Now how many times can one see this happen, and we've seen it at least a thousand times, before he becomes convinced that there is a high correlation between the ability to creep and the ability to read?

"And when one is convinced of this correlation between the abilities to creep and read, how long before one begins to wonder if somewhere in the world there is a people who, for one reason or another—social, cultural, religious—were never allowed on the ground as children. In other words, who were never permitted to crawl or creep. If there is such a culture, and if there is such a people, are those people able to read? Do you see what I mean?"

"I understand what you're saying," I reply, "but I don't know the answer."

"Neither do we," he says. "In the past months, members of the staff have thought about these things and discussed them past many midnights. You understand, these have been simple conversations. During them, we asked ourselves where might be the most likely place in the world that such a people might live?

"One might conjecture that this might be so around the equator because the ground itself would obviously be hostile to small children moving about on their hands and knees—there would be poisonous snakes, poisonous reptiles, poisonous plants and insects. And when one looks around the equator...

"As I sit here looking at that map in front of me," he says, "starting on the west coast of South America, I see the northern part of Peru, the southern part of Ecuador, and the headwaters of the Amazon. And then going in an easterly direction, I see the Mato Grosso of Brazil in the land south of the Amazon. Way across the Atlantic Ocean, I find myself in Nigeria, the Congo, Uganda, and them I continue farther on that band, and...

"Raymundo," he says, "I lost my place. Would you mind pointing to the equator for me so I can see where I'm talking about?"

"Of course," I say, getting up and walking over to the map.

The snare has been set, but by now I'm so interested in pointing to the places that he calls off that I'm not even aware that I am so congenially placing my foot inside.

"Farther east," he says, "I find Borneo, Sumatra, etcetera, etcetera, New Guinea. And then I say to myself, 'What do I know about the cultures in these places? How much civilization do I find in the headwaters of the Amazon? How much civilization do I find in the Xingu, in Niger, in Uganda, or the Congo, or Chad, or Borneo, or Sumatra?'

"This is an interesting question. In fact, Raymundo, I think it's a fascinating question—and it could be very, very important to the kids of the world.

"What great inventions were developed in these places? What cures for what diseases were discovered by the inhabitants of these places? What are the names of famous Brazilian natives there? What does an Ecuadorian name sound like in the jungles of Ecuador? We cannot answer these questions because we know so little about these places and even less about the people who live there.

"For instance," he says, "Raymundo, you are a citizen of Brazil. But how much do you know about the Amazon, or the Mato Grosso?"

"I know the Amazon is a very strong river," I reply. "I swim in it many times."

"Is that true?" he asks as if he doesn't believe his ears.

"Many times," I tell him. "In Para, I swim in the Amazon. It's a very strong river."

"No piranhas?"

"Not near Para," I answer. "Maybe farther upstream. One hears many stories." I pat my fat stomach. "I think maybe the piranhas come upstream if they know such a feast is there."

We have a little laugh.

"But what do you know about the Amazon as a region?" he asks.

"Not much. A lot of jungle."

"You have never been there?"

"I also have never stuck my head in a lion's mouth," I tell him. "The jungle is a dangerous place. I have enough trouble trying not to get hit by automobiles in the streets of Rio. Why would I want to tempt pythons and a thousand other dangers?"

"Is it so dangerous?" Glenn asks.

"Of course it is."

"How do you know?"

"I know," I tell him, "because I once saw this movie with Clark Gable and Joan Crawford, and it looked *very* dangerous to me."

"But that's only a movie," he says.

"You don't believe it?" I ask.

"Well, not all of it," he replies. "Hollywood exaggerates."

"I don't think Clark Gable would lie," I tell him.

He laughs, but I was not sure what he thinks so funny.

"And what about the natives?" he asks. "Do you know anything about them?"

"They're Indians," I answer. "They're very dangerous, too."

"How do you know that?"

"The Clark Gable movie..."

This time he laughs even harder, and I am beginning to get a little annoyed.

So Glenn changes the subject—or at least I think he changes it.

"Raymundo, when I was in your country, it was obvious to me that you know some very influential people. "

"I guess so," I say.

"In your last letter you said that your government would like me to come there and talk to some of the doctors about our work with brain-injured children."

"It would help our work so much, Glenn, if you could do this."

He stands up, walks to the map, and looks at the Mato Grosso for several minutes.

"If Carl Delacato and some other staff members and I will come to your country to talk about brain-injured children, do you think your friends would be so appreciative that they might arrange for us to see a primitive tribe?"

"I think so," I answer.

"Very well," he says. "You tell them that we will come to talk to the Brazilian doctors if they will arrange for us to go into the jungles."

"I will do as you ask," I tell him. "But I wish you would think this over. Your work is so important, and all the time you and Carl are in the jungle I will not sleep well because I will be worried about you."

"Then of course," he says, "you must come with us."

The trap is sprung. I am caught.

If my own father asked me to arrange for him to go into the jungle, I would make the arrangements and wave good-bye to him. But with Glenn Doman, I cannot do this. So with him and Carl Delacato and some other staff members, I go into the jungle, not once, but many times in the next few years. I even go to the Kalahari Desert and to Alaska. In fact, I go around the world with them to look at children.

I learn many things. The first thing I learn is not to trust Hollywood movies, even if Clark Gable and Joan Crawford are in them.

When people think of primitive tribes in Brazil, they are inclined to think of the Amazon region. But there are no primitive people along the Amazon. There are some hostile people, but no primitive ones. There have been civilized people up and down the Amazon for over three hundred years.

However, five hundred miles south of the Amazon there is an area called the Xingu Territory in the Mato Grosso. This is the largest inhabited territory that is unknown to the civilized world because it is unexplored.

The Brazilian government is happy to make arrangements for us to see a tribe of Indians. The Fund Centrale of Brazil, the agency responsible for the territory, provides transportation for us — an old DC-3 with a Brazilian Air Force crew. As I look at this little airplane, I know that I have taken leave of my senses.

The pilot is to fly us into the interior and there we will meet the Villas Boas brothers, Claudio and Orlando. We're told that the third brother, Leonardo, has recently died of a tropical disease (news that does not bolster my enthusiasm).

The story of the Villas Boas brothers is interesting indeed. Several years before, they had entered the Mato Grosso as government agents. They were to press the Xingu tribes deeper into the interior. But before long the brothers were dragging their feet — they had fallen in love with the Indians and were protecting their territories.

And soon, which is typical of the Brazilians, the Villas Boas brothers were on two payrolls: the Interior Department's to bring civilization into the jungle, and the Indian Protection Service's, to protect the Indians and hold the invaders back. These are obviously contradictory functions, though the Villas Boas brothers don't seem disturbed by the fact.

The Xingu tribes are composed of thirty to fifty people who thoroughly believe that they are the entire population of the world. Twenty miles away there may be another tribe of fifty people who speak a different language and have entirely different customs. Should the members of the two tribes meet, they could not understand each other.

Xinguanas are not stone-age people. They are possibly a thousand years more primitive than stone-age people and have no stone tools. They can't work stone; their arrowheads are made of bone.

Xinguanas are very handsome people and small in stature. The tallest is five feet. They are red in color, and the males are particularly well built. If you see a photo of a male Xinguana, you may think that he is seven feet tall because he is so superbly built. His hips are just wide enough to hold his legs on, and he has broad shoulders. If a Xinguana male stands next to me, I tower over him and I'm not tall — five feet, eight inches. When Dr. Evan Thomas accompanies us on an expedition (he is six feet, seven inches), the Xinguanas come eye-level with his belt buckle.

The Xinguanas' faces are oriental. Should you see a photo

of the faces of Xinguanas, Japanese, and Eskimos with no background of snow or the shoji screen or the flowering trees or the jungle, you would find it hard to tell one face from another.

The Xinguanas have a very complex speaking vocabulary composed almost entirely of nouns; they have no modifiers. For instance, because they do not have adjectives, they cannot say "a large, green leaf." Every leaf in their world has a name. If there are two leaves on a tree, a big one and little one, the Xinguanas will have a special name for the big leaf and a special name for the little leaf.

It seems as though the more primitive the people, the more complicated is their language. It has been said, for example, that the Eskimos have thirty words for snow but no one general word for snow. They have words for wet snow, dry snow, flowery snow, powdery snow, but no generic name for *snow*. So it is with the Xinguanas. They have no abstractions. They cannot count up to one. They have no God, either good or evil. And they do not have a measurement of time (which is the biggest abstraction of all).

Of course, we go to the Xinguanas with the idea of helping them. It never occurs to us that the Indians might have ideas that could help us.

We have the opportunity to live for many days with the Xinguanas and to see things that no civilized people have seen except the Villas Boas brothers and one or two others.

We civilized people think that one can equate primitiveness with hostility—all primitives are hostile. However, the fact is that it is just the opposite—primitives are extremely personable.

They treat us courteously as if we were equal, though of course by their standards we are not even men. They think we are all severely retarded since we're plainly incompetent as hunters, fishers, and food gatherers. Sometimes they treat us that way. If one of us should slip off into the jungle, in one minute there's an Indian behind him with a bow and arrow.

Obviously, the chief said, "Go watch over that idiot and see that he doesn't get himself killed." We later find the same thing true among the Eskimos.

Glenn and I often talk in the midst of the controversy unleashed on us by some professional societies, about how nice and peaceful it is in the Xingu. If it weren't such a burden on the Xinguanas, it might be nice to go live there.

Among these people, one finds no brain-injured children, and for a very simple reason. If a child is not like other children when he is born, he is simply buried. Disability is relative to civilization — the more civilized the society, the more disabled are its people. A society has to be very wealthy to support disabled people. Tiny tribes cannot do so, as they very well know.

By the way, if I tell you that disabled babies are buried, and if that sounds to you as though primitives don't love their children, rid yourself of that notion, because they adore their children. Their children are with them twenty-four hours a day, not only with them but on their bodies — literally on the mother's hip or her back or on the father's hip or on his back. Xinguana men take a very responsible position toward infants in their society.

The only two times I feel danger in the jungle are when we try to get the Indians to put their children on the ground so we can test their ability to crawl and creep. Both times, bows are flexed and spears are raised. In the Indians' eyes, we are threatening their children, which is certainly a good reason for even gentle people to become hostile.

We find that no Xinguana child has ever been allowed to crawl and creep on the ground. Babies are carried on their mothers' hips or backs. The Xinguanas have no written language.

And since that time, we've been around the world and have yet to find a truly primitive people who permit their babies to be on the ground.

What began as a question became an hypothesis. The

hypothesis became a theory. And now we have a great deal of empirical and scientific evidence that indicates that the theory is a fact. Not only is creeping an important level of development in a child's mobility, it is also terribly important in the child's visual development. In all the primitive people we have seen, the children are never allowed to creep, and none of them can focus his eyes on anything closer than arm's length. They are all far-sighted. We believe that when a child creeps, his near point vision is developed.

Glenn says, "If I am shown the *floor* of a culture, I can tell you if that culture has a written language or not. If the floor or the ground is conducive to children's creeping, then the chances are good that that culture has a written language. If the children are not allowed to creep, then it is doubtful that that culture has a written language. In order for people to write and to read, they must have developed the ability to focus their eyes on objects at a distance of about fifteen inches from their faces."

It's very important for the reader to understand the role the environment plays in the development of children. That's why I've brought in the Xinguanas. I love travelogues, but this trip was not a sightseeing venture. It was an expedition to further the knowledge about these interesting animals we call human beings.

In future chapters we will explore the effects that different environments have in the development of our children — how an excellent environment can develop superior children, how an average environment can develop average children, and how an inferior environment can develop inferior children. If these environments were unchangeable, such a consideration would be only an interesting mental excursion. However, since there *are* ways to enhance and improve a child's immediate environment and thereby improve his abilities, this information is important in determining how we can improve the early years development of not only brain-injured children and mongoloids but regular children as well. You will see. I will show you.

Since 1963, we have seen children all over the world — the Bushmen in the Kalahari Desert, Eskimos in Alaska, Navajos in Arizona. We have seen Samoan children, Russian children, French children. We have seen children where they live, and they have come from all parts of the world to see us at The Institutes in Philadelphia. During our 1970 travels, the documentary filmmaker, John Goodell, went with us. The result was a beautiful movie entitled *Always a New Beginning,* which was nominated for an Academy Award in 1974.

Today, that huge map on the wall of the board room at The Institutes recalls many memories. I can stand and look at it and relive, briefly, events of the last two decades. I am sure that no other people in the history of mankind have ever traveled so far to learn about how children grow. We do this not because we are in love with jet planes or dusty jeeps nor because we like to wade through jungle streams or stand in line at immigration counters. It is for the children that we do these things.

12

A Gentle Revolution

Between the years 1961 and 1964, ideas explode like bombs around us. But we're not only witnessing the birth of new ideas. We are coming upon some vital discoveries.

"Raymundo," Glenn says to me one day, "I have learned something truly astonishing about children."

I stop and listen carefully. I have now known Glenn for four years, and I have never heard him use the word *astonishing* before. He is a man with an abundant vocabulary who selects his words carefully.

"Have I ever told you about Tommy Lunski?" he asks.

"No," I shake my head.

"Well, when Tommy Lunski's parents brought him to The Institutes, he was really in bad shape—severely brain-injured. In fact, Mr. and Mrs. Lunski had been told that his condition was hopeless and he would never be better and that they should institutionalize him for life. Well, the Lunskis are of strong Polish stock, not much formal education. They own a small taproom."

"A what?"

"A taproom," he says. "A place that serves Scotch and whiskey and a lot of beer."

"Ah, a nightclub."

"More like a pub. Well, when we first saw Tommy, he was three years and two weeks old. He couldn't move, and he couldn't talk. He was really hurt. But his parents are great people — great, great, great. They did everything we told them to do. And Tommy got better *fast.*"

"Good," I say.

"Sure. Then after they had been on the program about a year, Tommy's parents started telling us things that we hadn't asked about. For instance, they told us that Tommy could read. In fact, they told us this so many times that we began to worry about them a little, because it seemed to us that they had this *thing* about his being able to read. We thought they were saying that he could make out a couple of words — *Look, Dick, look,* or that kind of thing. But you know what? Tommy Lunski could read *anything — Reader's Digest,* the encyclopedia, *Peyton Place,* you name it."

"That's good," I say.

"That's a helluva lot better than good," Glenn replies. "It's *astonishing!* Here's a kid who was counted out of the human race. Three medical advisors had said that Tommy would be a helpless idiot for the rest of his life. And now he is not only able to do the things that are expected of a normal four-year-old, he is able to do things *better* than most four-year-olds. Tommy can read! Not just little words — this kid can read *anything* and *everything!*"

"You're right," I reply. "That is astonishing."

Then he looks at me so straight and with such intensity that for a moment I feel uncomfortable. It's like someone is sending mental electricity through my body.

"Raymundo," he says very slowly and very clearly. *"All* kids can do this."

I thought about what he said and tried in my mind to understand how one piece of information led to such a conclusion.

"Don't you see?" Glenn says. "The only reason that Tommy can read is because someone showed him *how* to read. If we show little kids the secret, *all* of them can learn to read words as easily as they learn to hear words."

"Do you believe this?" I ask.

"I *know* this," he answers. "We now have all our kids at The Institutes on reading programs, and they are all learning to read."

Then I start to ask a foolish, foolish question. I start to ask, "If brain-injured kids can learn to read, how would that prove that average kids can learn?" I let that question sink in its own stupidity.

"That is truly astonishing," I admit.

I must remind the reader that this is back in 1961, in what one might call the dark ages. In 1961, most professionals think that little children cannot learn to read, that only genius children can pull such a trick. Those ages were dark, dark indeed. But Glenn is about to turn on the electric lights and tell the world that very young children not only *can* learn to read but that it is very good for them.

The staff members at The Institutes are eager to give the parents reading programs for their children. They feel those programs would be more successful if the parents had a booklet or a set of instructions. Because he can't get anyone else to write the booklet, Glenn sits down and writes it himself.

Sometimes things happen very quickly. The booklet becomes an article in the May 1963 *Ladies' Home Journal* entitled, "You Can Teach Your Baby to Read," and the article is expanded into a book published by Random House in 1964, entitled, *How to Teach Your Baby to Read*. The book becomes an instant hit, not only in the United States but in Great Britain, France, Italy, Germany, Japan, and Spain, to name only a few countries.

When the book appears on the market, many readers think that Glenn Doman is joshing, that he really doesn't mean *baby*. But, in fact, he *does mean baby*.

In essence, Glenn proposes that it is no more difficult for a child to learn to read a word than it is for him to learn to hear a word. He maintains that very young children are linguistic geniuses and that they will learn almost anything at an early age if it is presented to them in a clear, informative way.

For instance, all mothers teach their babies to hear and speak a foreign language. After all, no baby born in the United States automatically understands English, just as no baby born in Spain understands Spanish, and so forth. Mothers teach their children a language by speaking that language to them. If mothers waited until their children were of school age, the child would not be able to understand the language or to speak it. The baby has an insatiable urge to learn, and unless he is physically impaired, he will learn at a fantastic rate.

In reading about childhood geniuses (although they come from a variety of backgrounds and living conditions), time and again we find that they read before they went to school. We allow ourselves to assume that they were able to read at very early ages because they were geniuses. On the other hand, it is just as safe to assume that they became geniuses because they learned to read at a very early age.

One thing for sure, no genius in the history of the world taught himself to read — his mother, or his grandmother, or his Aunt Sarah had to say, "Look, kid, this is how it is done." Someone had to tell him the secret, just as someone had to tell him the secrets of the spoken word.

Glenn is right — reading words is no different than hearing words, except hearing is done with the ears and reading is done with the eyes. Yet in the past we hid the secrets of reading from young children. The schools have told us how clever we have to be and what elaborate training we need before we should dare take on this enormous task of trying to teach a child to read. Of course that's a lot of nonsense. The miracle of learning is not in the teacher—it's in the child. Before the child is five years of age, he can learn anything—one language, three languages, horseback riding, water skiing, anything—because his brain is growing at an enormous rate and he has no choice but to learn. It takes no special skill to turn a baby on to learning, on the contrary, it's terribly difficult to turn him off, because he *has* to learn. Over a million years of self-preservational instincts and a growing brain force him to learn in spite of himself, and in spite of how poorly we teach him!

We now realize that five-year-olds can learn faster than six-year-olds; that four-year-olds can learn faster than five-year-olds; and that one-year-olds can beat them all hands down, all because of early brain growth.

Most educators think Glenn's book is heresy, and they would love to burn both the book and its author at the stake. However, mothers buy the book by the thousands and begin to teach their babies to read by the thousands.

In the past, it has been hard for us to believe that children can learn so easily because there have been more myths about children than about the Greek and Roman gods. We have been told that children are nothing but little mimics who copy adults, and we have made a practice of keeping them in their place. "Children should be seen, not heard." Of course, we allowed them to be seen because they are so cute in their clumsiness, and they smile well.

If we want to justify our past errors by saying we did not know any better, then well and good. But in the light of present research and scientific information, what excuse can we now offer?

In the past we have taken an extremely dim view of children. For the most part we loved them and wanted them to be happy, but we also concluded that they were the way they were and nothing could be done about it. We were told by the professionals that children grew and matured in divinely ordained time frames and that there was little we could do to improve their lot. We were often told that tender loving care and a lot of patience would help them to be content with their inadequacies as they grew taller.

The educators told us that we could do irreparable harm if we tried to teach the child rather than just train him. They implied that each child was born with limitations on his capacity to learn, that his "intelligence quotient" was set at birth by certain genetic endowments, and that his learning potential could not be altered no matter what we did. To expect more from a child than mispronounced words and jumbled sentences might tend to frustrate him and mar his self-image for life.

We are now aware of the great tragedy in that advice. Studies show that the environment can alter the testable intelligence quotient by thirty points and more. We have become aware that the brain is like a computer; it will receive billions of pieces of information, and the more information it receives, the wider is its capacity to receive still more. We have seen that by age five, fact for fact, a child has eighty percent of all the knowledge he will ever acquire. We have seen that babies have the ability to be linguistic geniuses; they can learn three languages, six languages, with the same ease that they can learn one. It has been proposed that geniuses are not made in the womb but are the result of having the opportunity to learn at a very early age.

In recent years there has been a lot of talk about the *astonishing* learning capacity of children younger than five years of age. Now that many educators have come to this conclusion, they quickly claim that after years of study and analysis, they have come, not to Glenn Doman's conclusions, but to their *own*. Perhaps such actions verify what a *gentle revolution* Glenn's has been.

The truth is that eventually they *had* to come to these conclusions because Glenn is right.

The subtitle of *How to Teach Your Baby to Read* is "A Gentle Revolution." That revolution has taken place without any shell bursts, and the world has begun to look at very young children with new respect.

Growing a Child's Brain

How to Teach Your Baby to Read contains a secret that many mothers have discovered. In some of the thousands of letters that Glenn receives, mothers write, "I taught my three-year-old to read, and I noticed that when he learned to read his physical coordination improved." Or, "when my child learned to read, I think her hearing improved." Or, "when my child learned to read, his speech improved." Repeatedly, they ask, "Do you think there is any connection between the two?"

When Glenn shows me some of these letters, he says, "Look at how bright these women are. Aren't they great? They caught on. Of course the answer is yes in every case. And these women already know it."

Glenn continues, "Everything we do to alter one function of the brain has the potential to alter the other functions. But that's just part of the secret. The rest of the secret is that there is a good deal of research to indicate that we are not only improving the function of the brain, but we are actually *growing* the brain.

"Can you imagine the excitement that all mothers could have when teaching their young children if they knew that, not only were they turning their kid on to information, but at the same time they were actually growing their child's brain?"

Glenn is not saying that mothers are growing only that intangible thing called *mind*. Nor is he saying that they are growing only that intangible thing called *capacity for learning*. For besides growing both the mind and the learning capacity, scientific evidence indicates that they are also growing that physical thing called the brain.

As David Krech writes concerning his research with rats:

> This we do know: permitting the young IC (Isolated Control) rat to grow up in a psychologically impoverished environment creates an animal with a relatively deteriorated brain—a brain

with a relatively thin and light cortex, lowered blood supply, diminished enzymatic activities, smaller neuronal cell bodies, and fewer glia cells. A lack of adequate psychological fare for the young animal results in palpable, measurable, deteriorative changes in the brain's chemistry and anatomy.

Although we have worked only with rats, it is not unfair to ask whether our findings might also be applied to the human condition. Certainly we know that, among people, early cultural environments can range from the highly challenging to the severely impoverished. Although it would be scientifically unjustified to conclude at this stage that our results do apply to people, it would, I think, be socially criminal to assume that they do *not* apply — and, so assuming, fail to take account of the implication. [1]

When Dr. Krech was in Philadelphia in 1969 to receive the Human Potential Award from The Institutes in recognition for his work in advancing the knowledge of Mankind, Glenn asked him what conclusions he might have drawn from his work since that writing. Dr. Krech told him that he had established experiments in which rats received early stimulation in cages on moving platforms. When the researchers dissected these rats, not only were the quality of their brains better, but they were measurably larger and weighed more than did those of the rats that were not stimulated.

However, Dr. Krech said that they took these experiments one step further. Since he realized that the rats' ultimate function was that of a *searcher,* his staff built mazes and placed a third group of rats in those where they were allowed to search for food. The maze box did not move — only the rats moved through the corridors, finding their way. When these rats were dissected, the researchers found that their brains were even larger and heavier and were of better quality than those that were stimulated on the moving platforms. Dr. Krech said that these findings indicated that when members of a species were allowed or encouraged to perform their ultimate function, the

---

1. Krech, D.: In search of the engram. Med Op Rev 1:20, 1966a. Quoted LeWinn, E.B. (B.S., M.D., F.A.C.P.): *Human Neurological Organization.* Charles C. Thomas, Springfield, Illinois, 1969, p. 36.

size, quality, and weight of their brains could be increased.

Now what does this have to do with children? Dr. Krech says that if we want to look at humans and how these findings would apply to them, we should first consider what is a person's ultimate function. What one thing is a human capable of performing that is unique and his alone? The answer, Krech says, is obvious — language. Only we have language — a hearing, speaking, reading language. He says that if children have the opportunity and are encouraged to perform their ultimate function, utilizing that hearing, speaking, reading, writing language during the early stages of development, their brains will grow larger and heavier, and even the structural qualities will be improved.

Now, if you have a child under six years of age, doesn't this information make you want to run to where he is and take a look at his head? And when you look at his head, won't you be looking at it differently than you ever have before? First of all, you'll be looking at the confines of a potential genius. Now you know that although your child is smaller than you are, he can learn faster and learn more than you can ever hope to learn in the same amount of time.

If we view the brain as a computer, which it clearly is, then shouldn't we become more cautious about the information we feed into it? Of course we should.

Once, during a special lecture to a group of scientists, Glenn said that before the age of five a child's brain will indiscriminately accept any information as fact. He told them that computer experts have a good acronym to describe the process, "Gigo — garbage in, garbage out." Computer experts know that if wrong information is placed into a computer, one can expect wrong information to come out. In order to receive proper information from the computer, the wrong information must be cancelled. Doman stressed that the same is true with human beings — if wrong information is given to a child before he is five years of age, for the rest of his life he has to work to cancel erroneous concepts.

The scientists took exception to Glenn's statement and questioned its validity. So Glenn said, "Let me ask you a question, and you tell me the first answer that comes to your minds." Then he asked, "What is the moon made of?"

The room was filled with the scientists' laughter. They were convinced. Although some of the men present were employed in space exploration projects and had the most recent data in regard to the composition of the moon, the first answer that came to their minds was, *"Green cheese."*

We do not purposely lie to children. But we lie anyway. Sometimes we lie because we believe it does not really make any difference. Sometimes we lie because we think the children could not understand the information even if we told them. And sometimes we lie as a cover-up because we don't know the answer ourselves. The main reason we lie is that we have so little respect for children as individuals and so little regard for their potentials.

No matter how those scientists would like to eliminate that piece of nonsense from their brains, there is no way they can do it, because before they were five years old, a well-meaning aunt or uncle programmed their brains with a false piece of information. Now, for the rest of their lives, they will have to cancel that falsity before they can sort out facts.

Once we begin to look at the brain as a computer, we begin to look at infants differently. We begin to see them not as little ignorant blobs but as innocent and unprogrammed human beings. The real challenge is that each child has the potential of whatever we program him to be. There may well be the potential of genius inside every child's head.

In 1970, Glenn has some statements printed on balloons and gives those balloons to children throughout the world. One of the statements reads, "Compared to children, adults are hopelessly mentally retarded." When the words are translated to them, the children think the message is funny. Adults think it's amusing. But those who know better know that it is also true.

Teach Your Baby to Read

Perhaps the most important thing you can do with your baby is teach him to read. I strongly suggest that if you intend to do that, you get a copy of Glenn's *How to Teach Your Baby to Read* and discover what a joyous experience both you and your child can have together. In that book, Glenn offers a list of reasons why children should learn at an early age:

The earlier a child reads, the more he is likely to read, and the better he reads.

Some of the reasons, then, that children should learn to read when they are very young are as follows:

1. The hyperactivity of the two- and three-year-old child is, in fact, the result of a boundless thirst for knowledge. If he is given an opportunity to quench that thirst, at least for a small part of the time, he will be far less hyperactive, far easier to protect from harm, and far better able to learn about the world when he is moving about and learning about the physical world and himself.

2. The child's ability to take in information at two and three years of age will never be equaled again.

3. It is infinitely easier to teach a child to read at this age than it will ever be again.

4. Children taught to read at a very young age absorb a great deal *more information* than do children whose early attempts to learn are frustrated.

5. Children who learn to read while very young tend to comprehend better than youngsters who do not. It is interesting to listen to the three-year-old who reads with inflection and meaning, in contrast to the average seven-year-old, who reads each word separately and without appreciation of the sentence as a whole.

6. Children who learn to read while very young tend to read much more rapidly and comprehensively than children who do not. This is because young children are much less awed by reading and do not consider it a "subject" full of frightening abstractions. Tiny children view it as just another fascinating thing in a world jammed with fascinating things to be learned. They do not "hang up" on the details but deal with reading in a totally functional sense. They are very right to do so.

7. Finally, and at least as important as the above-stated reason — children love to learn to read at a very early age. [2]

Now you have become one of that select group who know—"Compared to children, adults *are* hopelessly mentally retarded." Now you know that you can alter not only the behavior of your child, but you can accelerate his brain growth.

As you look at your child's head, aren't you led to wonder how well you have ignited his learning capacity and how well you have grown those neurons encased within his skull? Doesn't the thought make you break out into a cold sweat, and isn't there a knot gnawing in the pit of your stomach? But when you think of all the possibilities that you now have to nurture your child's growth, doesn't it fill you with new excitement? It certainly should!

I do not want you to think for one moment that these are my ideas. I wish they were mine, but they are not. I have simply been honored to have been placed in such a position that I became aware of them. I have the pleasure to relate some of these findings. It should, by now, be clear that the man who assembled these bits of information from all parts of the world and from literally all efforts of scientific research is named Glenn Doman.

I soon return to Brazil, and the parents of my patients begin to teach their brain-injured children to read.

---

2. Doman, G.: (D.Sc.): *How to Teach Your Baby to Read.* Random House, New York, 1963, pp. 82, 83, 84.

Some of my distant colleagues hear that not only are we rehabilitating "hopeless" children to walk and talk better but are now teaching "mentally retarded" children to read.

"My God," they say to themselves, "maybe this man Veras has truly gone crazy."

Maybe they think my craziness is catching. They do not come close to see the progress we experience.

13

Vamos! Tempo e curto!

Our work is so important that there is no time to waste. My life becomes *Vamos! Tempo e curto!* "Let us hurry! Time is short!" I say this so often that some members of my staff begin to call me Dr. Vamos.

Sometimes I double the programs for the parents to do with their children because I realize that the faster a child improves, the better his chances are.

Glenn Doman tells me that I have the personality of an army general. I think maybe there is a gram of truth in his one-pound statement.

Children never get well soon enough for parents.
Parents ask, "How soon will our child be well?"
I reply, "How soon do you want your child to be well?"
"Would tomorrow be soon enough? How about tonight? How about now? Or six months ago? Or a year ago?"

I tell parents to pray for longer days so they can treat their child more.

It is our opinion that the single biggest favor we can do for parents is to push them without mercy. I am convinced that there is a correlation between *how soon* a child gets well and *if* he gets well.

We have parents who have treated their children for ten years and who have succeeded. But I think they are unusual, even extraordinary people. I do not believe that most people are capable of such long-term determination. I think most people are capable of huge sacrifices for reasonable periods of time but not for huge periods of time. I do not scorn them. I simply do not think it is in our nature to be capable of fierce enthusiasm for ten years at a stretch.

I think it is very important that parents be enthusiastic while their children are being programmed. It's important for the parents; it's important for the child. Once that enthusiasm wanes, the parents do the programs on sheer guts and determination, which is hundreds of times more difficult.

So I would rather push parents at a ferocious pace and get results as quickly as possible than set a slower pace, expecting slower results and trying to encourage the parents to be patient.

So I say, *"Vamos! Tempo e curto!"* "Let us hurry! Time is short!"

When time goes slowly and the results do not come quickly, parents begin to worry. They become afraid that I will give up on them and their child.

Sometimes a mother will come to me and say, "Oh, Dr. Veras, my child hasn't made much progress in the last month. Please don't give up on my child. I will work harder."

I tell her, "We will work harder, too."

Many times we see a child make nice progress and reach a new level of development, and then for maybe two or three months we see no change in him. These are terrible times for the parents.

Sometimes a mother will ask, "Dr. Veras, are you going to give up on my child now?"

I ask the mother, "When will you be ready to say to hell with your child?"

Without hesitation, the mother answers, "Never. Not until the day I die."

Then I tell her, "I will make a deal with you. I will give up the same day you do."

After these terrible times of waiting and hoping, the child will start to progress again. And then, only then, will we see the mother smile with all her heart. It is a privilege to witness the courage of these parents. At moments such as these, I am convinced that the Lord gives me the best part of the bargain.

When I first open my Institutes in Brazil, some medical people, without seeing our children, say that our claims are not true.

Sometimes these people come to see me and say, "We hear you make brain-injured children well. Prove it to us."

I spend much time with these people. I show them the children. I let them read the charts. I let them talk to the parents. Many times they look at all these things but they do not see.

They say, "Prove to us that their brains are injured." And I say, "What do I have to do? Cut the child's head open? His mother wouldn't like that."

And they look at the child who has made so much progress, and they ask, "How do you know he would not have been better even without your program?"

And I answer, "How many children do you see in institutions who get better without programs? How many children are institutionalized for one year or two years and are then released because they become well? If you look at this child's chart, you will see that five other doctors agreed that his condition was hopeless. I don't understand this. If I say there is hope for this child, I am told I have to prove it. Yet those five doctors could say there is no hope, and they did not have to prove their opinions. I do not understand why *hope* must have proof and *hopeless* needs only opinion."

Today, when these people come to me and ask about proof for this method of therapy, I ask them, "Do you have any other methods that work? If you have, show me *your* proof."

Of course they have no answer.

In the early days I also have many problems from the medical schools because they are so remote from new ideas. Medical students say, "We were not taught this way. Therefore, you must be wrong."

I tell them that they must sometimes look at their medical books as historical relics with many outdated references.

I am asked over and over, "Do you really *believe* it is possible to make brain-injured children well?" It's strange, this use of the word *believe*. They ask the question as one might ask, "Do you believe in a life hereafter?" They don't ask if I *know*— they ask if I *believe*. Very strange.

If a doctor tells a patient he has appendicitis and must have immediate surgery, the doctor is not asked if he *believes* this diagnosis to be true. It is assumed that he *knows* his work. But when we deal with the brain or the mind, people get nervous and make life miserable.

In the past, Glenn Doman has made a huge mistake by being far too generous with people who come to The Institutes in Philadelphia. These people say, "We have come to learn." And he tells them, "Stay and learn. We will feed you and give you a place to sleep." And because he has been so generous, these people often think to themselves, "He must be very rich," and they don't respect his generosity.

Glenn *is* rich, but not in money—he is rich in generosity. He is rich in ideas. And he is rich in genius.

I think people are suspicious of things they get for free. More often than not, they abuse the favors.

I tell Glenn, "You have no obligation to teach for free." He listens to me and promises never to do it again. And although he grows more cautious about potential leeches, I still see his eyes sparkle when people tell him that their only desire is to make brain-injured children well. However, so many times these people want to gain attention for themselves, not to serve the children.

I don't have time for such people. I used to spend so much time with these selfish nonthinkers, time I desperately needed in order to work with the children. Today, when these curious people come to me and tell me they want to see our work, I say to them, "First prove to me that you are really interested and that you are worthy of this information. If you prove to me that you are dedicated to the goal of making children well, then I will show you the results, and I will teach you everything I know. But if you do not prove to me that your intentions are honorable, then I have no obligation to tell you anything.

"If you want to come and learn, you are welcome, but don't think your presence is an honor for me or that it is an honor for the children.

"The children and I are not impressed by intentions or certificates or titles. We are impressed only by work and its results. My only obligation is to help make the children well. If you pay attention, it's easy to prove that our treatment is good."

I don't propose for one moment that all of our children become completely well. Of course we have failures. But not once has the staff ever blamed the children for these failures. We have failures because there is much we have yet to learn. We have failures because sometimes the parents do not carry out the program thoroughly. We have failures because we fail to make the parents understand. But these are our failures and the parents' failures—never the child's!

14

A Most Important
Piece of Paper

Aт this point, the reader might ask, "What does this man Veras think he is doing? Is he going to write a history of The Institutes for the Achievement of Human Potential, or a tribute to Glenn Doman? What does all this have to do with mongoloids?"

I answer, "Everything."

Now I would like very much to write the history of The Institutes for the Achievement of Human Potential. It would be both informative and entertaining, but I will never write this book because there is not time. In the present book I have told only things that are necessary for the reader to understand what I will later write about mongoloids.

If the reader would like a fuller account of The Institutes and its work with brain-injured children, I suggest that he read Glenn Doman's most recent book, *What to Do About Your Brain-Injured Child*. The reader would then see what a brief synopsis I have given.

Second, although I would love to write a tribute to Glenn Doman, I will never do this, nor would he ever expect me to do such a thing. All he has ever asked of me is my friendship and I have already given him that. As for the work I do with brain-injured children, Glenn would never presume to ask anyone to do his work for him. He knows full well that our work can, and often does, provide a one-way ticket to the poorhouse.

So if I first tell of the discoveries we have made about brain-injured children and neurological developments, it's to help the reader understand what I have to say about mongoloids. It will be like one-two-three. If I were to jump ahead and begin to tell about mongoloids at this point, it would be like one-three-two. The reader would have so many questions that he would not realize how simple these ideas really are.

However, if the reader understands everything in its turn, then all that I will say about mongoloids will be so simple. I promise.

In 1962, Glenn composed one of the most important papers in the history of the world. If this paper dealt only with the realities and the goals for brain-injured children, it would be important. But this paper deals with the neurological development of all children—brain-injured children, average children, genius children, mongoloid children, Catholic children, Protestant children, Jewish children, black children, white children, Oriental children, blind children, deaf children, crippled children, scholastic children, athletic children, short children, tall children, thin children, fat children, well-nourished children, undernourished children, crying children, laughing children—CHILDREN—the sons and daughters of men and women—KIDS—with running noses and galloping dreams—CHILDREN—our best hope for a better future.

Glenn realizes that proper goals must be established for our brain-injured children. Of course there have been many goals devised for each and every one of these children. They were good goals. For instance, a mother who had a blind child wanted her child to see. A mother of a paralyzed child wanted her child to move. The mother of a speechless child wanted her child to speak. And the mother of a functionally deaf child wanted her child to hear.

The goals seemed to be clear cut and well defined. Often, as the children's condition improved, the goals were altered and redefined.

"A mother would tell me," Glenn says, "'If my child could hear just one sound, I'd be happy.' Or, 'If my child could just crawl across the floor, I'd be happy.'

"At the time, these mothers meant what they said. But months later, when the child can crawl across the floor, the mother seems pleased but not overly impressed. Now, her qualifications for happiness have changed. 'If he could only creep on his hands and knees, then I'd be happy.' Later, when we would see that kid creeping, she says, 'Yes, that's pretty good, but when is he going to walk?' These mothers drove us crazy with their slide-rule conditions for happiness. Finally we have a real confrontation. The mother enters my office showing that she is annoyed. I ask what the problem is and she says, 'Johnny's been walking for six months, but he still hasn't won one footrace!'

"I would go home at night and think, 'Good God, what's the matter with that mother? What the hell does she expect? Will she ever be happy?' I even started believing all those nasty things they were saying about mothers, that there really is no way to please them. But then after one of these experiences, I said aloud to myself, 'That woman is not going to be pleased even if that kid can do everything that every other kid can do. She's not going to be happy until he's *better* than other kids.' Then I stopped cold and realized that that was exactly right. And wasn't that kid lucky to have such a mother.

"So," Glenn says, "I realized that the goal we had to establish for each brain-injured child would have to be *nor-*

mality, because mothers weren't going to be happy with anything less. Nor should they be."

Glenn thinks it should be a simple task to find out the
normal pattern of development of a child. A five-minute trip
to the library, a glance into the card catalog, and there will be
a book called *The Normal Development of Children.*

He soon finds there is no such book. He finds voluminous
entries on *The Disturbed Sibling Versus the Only Child, The
Potty Training of Blue-Eyed Infants, The Socio-psychological
Adjustments of Siamese Twins,* and *Growing Up with a
Guatemalan Bucktoothed Refugee.* And he finds baby books
filled with cutesy stuff such as "first trip to grandmother's,"
"first birthday present from Aunt Jane." Only occasionally does
he find a mention of the really important levels of child development—a reference to the child's "preference of handed-
ness" or the age at which a child takes his first steps. He finds
the same to be true in "doctor's-advice-to-mothers" books—
long sections on teething and drooling and diaper rash but few
statements of, "These are the things you should expect your
child to do, and these are the ages when he should do them."

So Glenn decides that if there is going to be a proper tool
with which to compare the neurological development of a child
with the norm, he is going to have to design that tool. And that is
exactly what he does. That paper—that tool—is called *The
Doman-Delacato Developmental Profile.*

In the following pages I present *The Doman-Delacato
Developmental Profile* at length because it is so important. It is
the story of children's lives, *all* children's. It tells clearly how
children develop from birth to seventy-two months.

In his book *Human Neurological Organization,* Dr.
Edward B. LeWinn writes:

> *The Doman-Delacato Developmental Profile* is a diagnostic
> instrument in that it readily detects the presence of neurological
> dysorganization. It clearly defines the degree and extent to which
> neurological dysorganization is present as well as the functional

level of involvement. . . . It also determines the position of the un-
impaired child in the range of normality, that is, whether his
development is slow, average, or superior. [3]

"*The Doman-Delacato Developmental Profile* serves as a
model of human development in a number of ways," says
Gretchen Kerr, Director of the Children's Institute of the
Institutes for the Achievement of Human Potential.

First, it is divided into the *sensory* side of vision (seeing), auditory (hearing), and tactile (feeling), which are the pathways
through which information about the environment goes into the
brain, and the *motor* side of mobility, language, and manual
competence (hand function), which are the pathways through
which the brain can respond to the environment.

Second, the *Profile* serves as a model of the sequence in which
the brain matures and the time in which this occurs.

Third, it serves as a model of the sequence of development of
specific functions that a human being should accomplish to
achieve complete neurological development. [4]

I have the feeling that there will be many mothers who will
quickly turn the pages to find the areas where she can compare
her child's development. Then she may read to find what is the
next level of development she can expect or encourage. I
consider that cheating. However, I am not opposed to mothers'
cheating in regard to improving the lot of their children.

I am not going to tell you that you must read every word or
your child's life may be in danger, but I am going to suggest that
if you first read all the stages of the *Profile* before looking up
your child's development, you may have a better and more
complete picture of these fascinating creatures we call infants,
babies, and children.

But first let me warn you of two things:

First, don't be surprised if there are few or no surprises. I

3. LeWinn, E.B. (B.S., M.D., F.A.C.P.): *Human Neurological Organization.*
Charles C. Thomas, Springfield, Illinois, 1969, p. 204.

4. Kerr, G.: Parent Orientation Lecture, The Institutes for the Achievement of
Human Potential, Philadelphia, Pa., 1973.

have noticed that when the *Profile* is presented to mothers, they tend to say, "Of course that's true, that's exactly how children grow." Since the *Profile* reflects the average development of children, that is precisely what their reactions should be.

Second, *The Doman-Delacato Developmental Profile* is a statement of how things are under the present conditions, which have been generally accepted in the rearing of children. However, it is not a statement that those conditions are unchangeable. As most mothers will quickly realize, the *Profile*, like brain growth, is not a static and irrevocable pattern but an adjustable slide rule.

Thousands of mothers throughout the world have already adjusted that slide rule by teaching their babies to read, and they have accelerated the development of their children. In several studies, it has been found that when infants are placed in a poor neurological environment, they progress at slower rates. As you explore these levels of children's development, the most important thing for you to remember is that there is a good deal of scientific and empirical evidence that the abilities and the neurological organization of children are a direct reflection of the environment we have created for them in their early years. Many of these conditions can be altered if we wish to alter them. Children can be brighter and more active if we wish to make their environment more conducive to producing brighter and more active children.

The Doman-Delacato Developmental Profile [5] (*chart 1*)

VISUAL COMPETENCE (*chart 2*)

The First Developmental Level of a child's visual competence is *light reflex*. At birth babies are functionally blind, but their eyes respond immediately to a bright light by the pupils' dilating reflexively. When the light is taken away, the pupils

---

5. *The Doman-Delacato Developmental Profile:* Glenn J. Doman, The Institutes for the Achievement of Human Potential, Philadelphia, Pa., 1962. Modified 1964, 1971.

Chart 1: The Doman-Delacato Developmental Profile

BRAIN STAGE		TIME FRAME	VISUAL COMPETENCE	AUDITORY COMPETENCE	TACTILE COMPETENCE
VII	SOPHISTI-CATED CORTEX	Superior 36 Mon. Average 72 Mon. Slow 108 Mon.	Reading words using a dominant eye consistent with the dominant hemisphere	Understanding of 2000 words and simple sentences	Tactile identification of objects using a hand consistent with hemispheric dominance
VI	PRIMITIVE CORTEX	Superior 22 Mon. Average 36 Mon. Slow 70 Mon.	Identification of visual symbols and letters within experience	Understanding of complete vocabulary and proper sentences with proper ear	Description of objects by tactile means
V	EARLY CORTEX	Superior 13 Mon. Average 18 Mon. Slow 36 Mon.	Differentiation of similar but unlike simple visual symbols	Understanding of 10 to 25 words and two word couplets	Tactile differentiation of similar but unlike objects
IV	INITIAL CORTEX	Superior 8 Mon. Average 12 Mon. Slow 22 Mon.	Convergence of vision resulting in simple depth perception	Understanding of two words of speech	Tactile understanding of the third dimension in objects which appear to be flat
III	MIDBRAIN	Superior 4 Mon. Average 7 Mon. Slow 12 Mon.	Appreciation of detail within a configuration	Appreciation of meaningful sounds	Appreciation of gnostic sensation
II	PONS	Superior 1 Mon. Average 2.5 Mon. Slow 4 Mon.	Outline perception	Vital response to threatening sounds	Perception of vital sensation
I	MEDULLA and CORD	Superior Birth to .5 Average Birth to 1.0 Slow Birth to 1.5	Light reflex	Startle reflex	Babinski reflex

THE DOMAN-DELACATO DEVELOPMENTAL PROFILE BY GLENN J. DOMAN CARL H. DELACATO ED. D. ROBERT J. DOMAN M.D.	MOBILITY	LANGUAGE	MANUAL COMPETENCE
	Using a leg in a skilled role which is consistent with the dominant hemisphere	Complete vocabulary and proper sentence structure	Using a hand to write which is consistent with the dominant hemisphere
	Walking and running in complete cross pattern	2000 words of language and short sentences	Bimanual function with one hand in a dominant role
	Walking with arms freed from the primary balance role	10 to 25 words of language and two word couplets	Cortical opposition bilaterally and simultaneously
	Walking with arms used in a primary balance role most frequently at or above shoulder height	Two words of speech used spontaneously and meaningfully	Cortical opposition in either hand
	Creeping on hands and knees, culminating in cross pattern creeping	Creation of meaningful sounds	Prehensile grasp
	Crawling in the prone position culminating in cross pattern crawling	Vital crying in response to threats to life	Vital release
THE INSTITUTES FOR THE ACHIEVEMENT OF HUMAN POTENTIAL 8801 STENTON AVENUE PHILADELPHIA, PA. 19118	Movement of arms and legs without bodily movement	Birth cry and crying	Grasp reflex

THIS MAY NOT BE REPRODUCED IN WHOLE OR IN PART WITHOUT SPECIAL PERMISSION OF GLENN J. DOMAN, 8801 STENTON AVENUE, PHILADELPHIA, PENNSYLVANIA 19118, U.S.A. © 1962. MODIFIED 1964, 1971.

Chart 2: Visual Competence

BRAIN STAGE		TIME FRAME	VISUAL COMPETENCE
VII	SOPHISTI-CATED CORTEX	Superior 36 Mon. Average 72 Mon. Slow 108 Mon.	Reading words using a dominant eye consistent with the dominant hemisphere
VI	PRIMITIVE CORTEX	Superior 22 Mon. Average 36 Mon. Slow 70 Mon.	Identification of visual symbols and letters within experience
V	EARLY CORTEX	Superior 13 Mon. Average 18 Mon. Slow 36 Mon.	Differentiation of similar but unlike simple visual symbols
IV	INITIAL CORTEX	Superior 8 Mon. Average 12 Mon. Slow 22 Mon.	Convergence of vision resulting in simple depth perception
III	MIDBRAIN	Superior 4 Mon. Average 7 Mon. Slow 12 Mon.	Appreciation of detail within a configuration
II	PONS	Superior 1 Mon. Average 2.5 Mon. Slow 4 Mon.	Outline perception
I	MEDULLA and CORD	Superior Birth to .5 Average Birth to 1.0 Slow Birth to 1.5	Light reflex

dilate. This will occur as often as the light is presented and removed.

The Second Development Level of a child's visual competence is *outline perception*. At this stage the baby begins to see silhouettes of people and objects.

If a baby has outline perception at 2.5 months, his development of visual competence is rated *average*.

If a baby has outline perception at 1 month, his development of visual competence is rated *superior*.

If a baby does *not* have outline perception until 4 months, his development of visual competence is rated *slow*.

The Third Developmental Level of a child's visual competence is *appreciation of detail within a configuration*. Now the baby begins to see the mother's face rather than just a shadowy outline and can see a painted design on a plastic cup instead of just the gross outline of the object.

If a baby has an appreciation of detail within a configuration at 7 months, his development of visual competence is rated *average*.

If a baby has an appreciation of detail within a configuration at 4 months, his development of visual competence is rated *superior*.

If a baby does *not* have an appreciation of detail within a configuration until he is 12 months, his development of visual competence is rated *slow*.

The Fourth Developmental Level of a child's visual competence is *convergence of vision resulting in simple depth perception*. Now the child can co-ordinate his eyes to focus on an object and blend the images received by both eyes, and he can realize that objects have depth as well as height and width.

If a child has convergence of vision resulting in simple depth perception at 12 months, his development of visual competence is rated *average*.

If a child has convergence of vision resulting in simple depth perception at 8 months, his development of visual competence is rated *superior*.

If a child does *not* have convergence of vision resulting in simple depth perception until 22 months, his development of visual competence is rated *slow*.

The Fifth Developmental Level of a child's visual competence is *differentiation of similar but unlike simple visual symbols*. Although on a printed page a red ball and a red apple may appear to be similar, the child can now recognize the difference between the two.

If a child can differentiate between similar but unlike simple visual symbols at 18 months, his development of visual competence is rated *average*.

If a child can differentiate between similar but unlike simple visual symbols at 13 months, his development of visual competence is rated *superior*.

If a child *cannot* differentiate between similar but unlike simple visual symbols until 36 months, his development of visual competence is rated *slow*.

The Sixth Developmental Level of a child's visual competence is *identification of visual symbols and letters within experience*. Now a child can recognize some of the letters of the alphabet, triangles, circles, or even printed words (if, of course, he has had the opportunity of someone's telling him what they are or has been able to draw conclusions from experience).

If a child can identify visual symbols and letters within his experience at 36 months, his development of visual competence is rated *average*.

If a child can identify visual symbols and letters within his experience at 22 months, his development of visual competence is rated *superior*.

If a child *cannot* identify visual symbols and letters within his experience until 70 months, his development of visual competence is rated *slow.*

The Seventh Developmental Level of a child's visual competence is *reading words using a dominant eye consistent with the dominant hemisphere.* One eye is a leader; one eye is a follower. If a child is using his right eye as the leader, the chances are good that his left brain hemisphere is dominant. If his neurological development is proper, he is right-eyed, right-eared, right-handed, and right-footed. Or he may be consistently left-sided; it makes little difference so long as one side is consistently dominant.

If a child can read words using a dominant eye consistent with the dominant hemisphere at 72 months, his development of visual competence is rated *average.*

If a child can read words using a dominant eye consistent with the dominant hemisphere at 36 months, his development of visual competence is rated *superior.*

If a child *cannot* read words using a dominant eye consistent with the dominant hemisphere until 108 months, his development of visual competence is rated *slow.*

AUDITORY COMPETENCE (*chart 3*)

The First Developmental Level of a child's auditory competence is *startle reflex,* which is present at birth. If there is a loud, sharp noise close by, the baby will react with a jerk, and he will react in the same manner as often as the noise is made.

The Second Developmental Level of a child's auditory competence is *vital response to threatening sounds.* Now, when the baby hears harsh, loud noises, he will cry, thus sounding his alarm system to alert his mother.

If a child has a vital response to threatening sounds as 2.5 months, his development of auditory competence is rated *average.*

Chart 3: Auditory Competence

BRAIN STAGE		TIME FRAME	AUDITORY COMPETENCE
VII	SOPHISTI-CATED CORTEX	Superior 36 Mon. Average 72 Mon. Slow 108 Mon.	Understanding of complete vocabulary and proper sentences with proper ear
VI	PRIMITIVE CORTEX	Superior 22 Mon. Average 36 Mon. Slow 70 Mon.	Understanding of 2000 words and simple sentences
V	EARLY CORTEX	Superior 13 Mon. Average 18 Mon. Slow 36 Mon.	Understanding of 10 to 25 words and two word couplets
IV	INITIAL CORTEX	Superior 8 Mon. Average 12 Mon. Slow 22 Mon.	Understanding of two words of speech
III	MIDBRAIN	Superior 4 Mon. Average 7 Mon. Slow 12 Mon.	Appreciation of meaningful sounds
II	PONS	Superior 1 Mon. Average 2.5 Mon. Slow 4 Mon.	Vital response to threatening sounds
I	MEDULLA and CORD	Superior Birth to .5 Average Birth to 1.0 Slow Birth to 1.5	Startle reflex

If a child has a vital response to threatening sounds at 1 month, his development of auditory competence is rated *superior*.

If a child does *not* have a vital response to threatening sounds until 4 months, his development of auditory competence is rated *slow*.

The Third Developmental Level of a child's auditory competence is *appreciation of meaningful sounds*. Now the baby begins to respond to the mother's voice and to pleasant sounds as well as harsh noises. He begins to realize which is which.

If a baby has appreciation of meaningful sounds at 7 months, his development of auditory competence is rated *average*.

If a baby has appreciation of meaningful sounds at 4 months, his development of auditory competence is rated *superior*.

If a baby does *not* have appreciation of meaningful sounds until 12 months, his development of auditory competence is rated *slow*.

The Fourth Developmental Level of a child's auditory competence is *understanding of two words of speech*. What is the best way for a mother to test when a baby understands two words of speech? If a mother *thinks* her baby understands two words, you can believe her. She knows.

If a child has an understanding of two words of speech at 12 months, his development of auditory competence is rated *average*.

If a child has an understanding of two words of speech at 8 months, his development of auditory competence is rated *superior*.

If a child does *not* have an understanding of two words of speech until 22 months, his development of auditory competence is rated *slow*.

The Fifth Developmental Level of a child's auditory competence is *an understanding of 10 to 25 words and 2-word couplets*.

If a child has an understanding of 10 to 25 words and 2-word couplets at 18 months, his development of auditory competence is rated *average*.

If a child has an understanding of 10 to 25 words and 2-word couplets at 13 months, his development of auditory competence is rated *superior*.

If a child does *not* have an understanding of 10 to 25 words and 2-word couplets until 36 months, his development of auditory competence is rated *slow*.

The Sixth Developmental Level of a child's auditory competence is *an understanding of 2000 words and simple sentences.* Once you realize that your child understands more words than you care to count, you know that chances are he has reached the 2000 mark, and of course you realize whether he understands simple sentences.

If a child has an understanding of 2000 words and simple sentences at 36 months, his development of auditory competence is rated *average*.

If a child has an understanding of 2000 words and simple sentences at 18 months, his development of auditory competence is rated *superior*.

If a child does *not* have an understanding of 2000 words and simple sentences until 70 months, his development of auditory competence is rated *slow*.

The Seventh Developmental Level of a child's auditory competence is *an understanding of complete vocabulary and proper sentences with proper ear.* Now you have to close the door if you want to say anything you do not want him to repeat or tell the neighbors. If he is consistently right-eyed, right-handed, right-footed, he should also be right-eared. If he tries to listen to soft sounds, such as a watch ticking, he will consistently place the object to his right ear.

If a child has an understanding of complete vocabulary and proper sentences with proper ear at 72 months, his development of auditory competence is rated *average*.

If a child has an understanding of complete vocabulary and proper sentences with proper ear at 36 months, his development of auditory competence is rated *superior*.

If a child does *not* have an understanding of complete vocabulary and proper sentences with proper ear until 108 months, his development of auditory competence is rated *slow*.

TACTILE COMPETENCE (*chart 4*)

The First Developmental Level of a child's tactile competence are the *skin reflexes*. There are a number of such reflexes present at birth. The *Profile* measures the Babinski reflex. This reflex occurs when the outside of the sole is stroked from heel to toe. The baby's big toe should flex upward and the other toes fan out.

The Second Developmental Level of a child's tactile competence is the *perception of vital sensation*. At this stage of development the baby begins to feel pain acutely and will cry if hungry or hurt in some way.

If a child has perception of vital sensation at 2.5 months, his development of tactile competence is rated *average*.

If a child has perception of vital sensation at 1 month, his development of tactile competence is rated *superior*.

If a child does *not* have perception of vital sensation until 4 months, his development of tactile competence is rated *slow*.

The Third Developmental Level of a child's tactile competence is *appreciation of gnostic sensation*. Now the baby's tactility has become more refined; he responds to more subtle sensation, such as warm versus cool.

If a baby has appreciation of gnostic sensation at 7 months, his development of tactile competence is rated *average*.

If a baby has appreciation of gnostic sensation at 4 months,

Chart 4: Tactile Competence

BRAIN STAGE		TIME FRAME	TACTILE COMPETENCE
VII	SOPHISTI-CATED CORTEX	Superior 36 Mon. Average 72 Mon. Slow 108 Mon.	Tactile identification of objects using a hand consistent with hemispheric dominance
VI	PRIMITIVE CORTEX	Superior 22 Mon. Average 36 Mon. Slow 70 Mon.	Description of objects by tactile means
V	EARLY CORTEX	Superior 13 Mon. Average 18 Mon. Slow 36 Mon.	Tactile differentiation of similar but unlike objects
IV	INITIAL CORTEX	Superior 8 Mon. Average 12 Mon. Slow 22 Mon.	Tactile understanding of the third dimension in objects which appear to be flat
III	MIDBRAIN	Superior 4 Mon. Average 7 Mon. Slow 12 Mon.	Appreciation of gnostic sensation
II	PONS	Superior 1 Mon. Average 2.5 Mon. Slow 4 Mon.	Perception of vital sensation
I	MEDULLA and CORD	Superior Birth to .5 Average Birth to 1.0 Slow Birth to 1.5	Babinski reflex

his development of tactile competence is rated *superior*.

If a baby does *not* have appreciation of gnostic sensation until 12 months, his development of tactile competence is rated *slow*.

The Fourth Developmental Level of a child's tactile competence is *tactile understanding of the third dimension in objects which appear to be flat*. In other words, a penny on a tabletop may visually appear flat, but by touch the child can realize that it is three-dimensional.

If a child has tactile understanding of the third dimension at 12 months, his development of tactile competence is *average*.

If a child has tactile understanding of the third dimension at 8 months, his development of tactile competence is rated *superior*.

If a child does *not* have tactile understanding of the third dimension until 22 months, his development of tactile competence is rated *slow*.

The Fifth Developmental Level of a child's tactile competence is *tactile differentiation of similar but unlike objects*. In other words, he can tell, by feeling but not seeing, an apple from a ball, or a spoon from a fork.

If a child by touch alone can differentiate between similar but unlike objects at 18 months, his development of tactile competence is rated *average*.

If a child by touch alone can differentiate between similar but unlike objects at 13 months, his development of tactile competence is rated *superior*.

If a child by touch alone *cannot* differentiate between similar but unlike objects until 36 months, his development of tactile competence is rated *slow*.

The Sixth Developmental Level of a child's tactile competence is *description of objects by tactile means*. Now the child can feel objects and discern what they look like without seeing them.

If a child can describe objects by tactile means at 36 months, his development of tactile competence is rated *average*.

If a child can describe objects by tactile means at 22 months, his development of tactile competence is rated *superior*.

If a child *cannot* describe objects by tactile means until 70 months, his development of tactile competence is rated *slow*.

The Seventh Developmental Level in a child's tactile competence is *tactile identification of objects using a hand consistent with hemispheric dominance*. Now the child should be able to identify almost any object within his experience by feeling it without having to look at it. Dimes, quarters, marbles, grapes, pearls, pencils, crayons, and so forth. He should consistently use his right hand if he is right-eyed, right-eared, and right-footed. Again, it makes little difference if the child is left-sided or right-sided as long as the sidedness is consistent.

If a child can identify objects using a hand consistent with hemispheric dominance at 72 months, his development of tactile competence is rated *average*.

If a child can identify objects using a hand consistent with hemispheric dominance at 36 months, his development of tactile competence is rated *superior*.

If a child *cannot* identify objects using a hand consistent with hemispheric dominance until 108 months, his development of tactile competence is rated *slow*.

MOBILITY COMPETENCE (*chart 5*)

The First Developmental Level of a child's mobility competence is movement of arms and legs without body movement. The baby can kick and move his arms, but this movement does not propel him in any direction. This capability is present at birth.

The Second Developmental Level of a child's mobility competence is *crawling in the prone position culminating in a*

Chart 5: Mobility Competence

BRAIN STAGE		TIME FRAME	MOBILITY
VII	SOPHISTI-CATED CORTEX	Superior 36 Mon. Average 72 Mon. Slow 108 Mon.	Using a leg in a skilled role which is consistent with the dominant hemisphere
VI	PRIMITIVE CORTEX	Superior 22 Mon. Average 36 Mon. Slow 70 Mon.	Walking and running in complete cross pattern
V	EARLY CORTEX	Superior 13 Mon. Average 18 Mon. Slow 36 Mon.	Walking with arms freed from the primary balance role
IV	INITIAL CORTEX	Superior 8 Mon. Average 12 Mon. Slow 22 Mon.	Walking with arms used in a primary balance role most frequently at or above shoulder height
III	MIDBRAIN	Superior 4 Mon. Average 7 Mon. Slow 12 Mon.	Creeping on hands and knees, culminating in cross pattern creeping
II	PONS	Superior 1 Mon. Average 2.5 Mon. Slow 4 Mon.	Crawling in the prone position culminating in cross pattern crawling
I	MEDULLA and CORD	Superior Birth to .5 Average Birth to 1.0 Slow Birth to 1.5	Movement of arms and legs without bodily movement

cross pattern. At this stage the child begins to move about on the floor. At first the random use of arms and legs will propel the baby forward. As he gains more skill in moving, the cross pattern (right arm, left leg, then left arm, right leg) will emerge.

If a child is crawling at 2.5 months, his development of mobility competence is rated *average.*

If a child is crawling at 1 month, his development of mobility competence is rated *superior.*

If a child does *not* crawl until 4 months, his development of mobility competence is rated *slow.*

The Third Developmental Level of a child's mobility competence is *creeping on hands and knees culminating in a cross pattern.* Often upon first creeping a child moves left leg with left hand and right leg with right hand, but he should soon develop a cross pattern—left leg moving forward with right hand, right leg moving forward with left hand.

If a child is creeping on hands and knees culminating in a cross pattern at 7 months, his mobility development is rated *average.*

If a child is creeping on hands and knees culminating in a cross pattern at 4 months, his mobility development is rated *superior.*

If a child is *not* creeping on hands and knees culminating in a cross pattern until 12 months, his mobility development is rated *slow.*

The Fourth Developmental Level of a child's mobility competence is *walking with arms used in a primary balance role most frequently at or above shoulder height.* At this level the child uses his arms to aid his balance; he weaves back and forth, walking from one place to another. He is often called a toddler at this stage.

If a child is walking with arms in a primary balance role at 12 months, his mobility development is rated *average.*

If a child is walking with arms in a primary balance role at 8 months, his mobility development is rated *superior*.

If a child is *not* walking with arms in a primary balance role until 22 months, his mobility development is rated *slow*.

The Fifth Developmental Level of a child's mobility competence is *walking with arms freed from the primary balance role*. Now his hands have lowered, and they are not held out for help in balancing.

If a child is walking with arms freed from the primary balance role at 18 months, his mobility development is rated *average*.

If a child is walking with arms freed from the primary balance role at 13 months, his mobility development is rated *superior*.

If a child is *not* walking with arms freed from the primary balance role until 36 months, his mobility development is rated *slow*.

The Sixth Developmental Level of a child's mobility competence is *walking and running in complete cross pattern*. Now his left hand moves forward as his right foot moves forward, and his right hand moves forward with the left foot.

If a child is walking and running in complete cross pattern at 36 months, his development is rated *average*.

If a child is walking and running in complete cross pattern at 22 months, his mobility development is rated *superior*.

If a child is *not* walking and running in complete cross pattern until 70 months, his mobility development is rated *slow*.

The Seventh Developmental Level of a child's mobility competence is *using a leg in a skilled role consistent with the dominant hemisphere* (kicking a ball, stepping up onto a stool, etc.). This is not as complicated as it sounds. If it is obvious that your child is right-handed, right-eyed, right-eared, and right-footed, then his dominant hemisphere is the left brain.

Remember, the left brain controls the right side of the body, and the right brain controls the left side. If a child's dominance is developed at this level, he will consistently be right-handed, right-footed, right-eyed, and right-eared. Of course, he could be left-handed, left-footed, left-eyed, and left-eared. But it is important that he be *consistently* one or the other. The side is not important — the consistency is.

If a child is using a leg in a skilled role consistent with the dominant hemisphere at 72 months, his mobility development is rated *average*.

If a child is using a leg in a skilled role consistent with the dominant hemisphere at 36 months, his mobility development is rated *superior*.

If a child is *not* using a leg in a skilled role consistent with the dominant hemisphere until 108 months, his mobility development is rated *slow*.

LANGUAGE (*chart 6*)

The First Developmental Level of a child's language is *birth cry and crying*. This means that he cries at birth.

The Second Developmental Level of a child's language is *vital crying in response to threats to life*. In other words, the baby hears a harsh sound or is stuck by a pin, and in response he cries in a more insistent way than at the previous stage.

If a baby has vital crying in response to threats to life at 2.5 months, his language development is rated *average*.

If a baby has vital crying in response to threats to life at 1 month, his language development is rated *superior*.

If a baby does *not* have vital crying in response to threats to life until 4 months, his language development is rated *slow*.

The Third Developmental Level of a child's language is *creation of meaningful sounds*. This stage goes beyond cooing

Chart 6: Language

BRAIN STAGE		TIME FRAME	LANGUAGE
VII	SOPHISTI-CATED CORTEX	Superior 36 Mon. Average 72 Mon. Slow 108 Mon.	Complete vocabulary and proper sentence structure
VI	PRIMITIVE CORTEX	Superior 22 Mon. Average 36 Mon. Slow 70 Mon.	2000 words of language and short sentences
V	EARLY CORTEX	Superior 13 Mon. Average 18 Mon. Slow 36 Mon.	10 to 25 words of language and two word couplets
IV	INITIAL CORTEX	Superior 8 Mon. Average 12 Mon. Slow 22 Mon.	Two words of speech used spontaneously and meaningfully
III	MIDBRAIN	Superior 4 Mon. Average 7 Mon. Slow 12 Mon.	Creation of meaningful sounds
II	PONS	Superior 1 Mon. Average 2.5 Mon. Slow 4 Mon.	Vital crying in response to threats to life
I	MEDULLA and CORD	Superior Birth to .5 Average Birth to 1.0 Slow Birth to 1.5	Birth cry and crying

and gurgling. The mother begins to realize that the baby's sounds communicate how he feels, and certain sounds become consistent.

If a baby is creating meaningful sounds at 7 months, his language development is rated *average*.

If a baby is creating meaningful sounds at 4 months, his language development is rated *superior*.

If a baby is *not* creating meaningful sounds until 12 months, his language development is rated *slow*.

The Fourth Developmental Level of a child's language is *two words of speech used spontaneously and meaningfully.* *Mama, Dada,* and *baba* for bottle will suffice. The mother recognizes a word rather than a consistent sound. No matter what the two words are, this is a joyful level because the child has broken the code and is beginning to understand what language is.

If a child is saying two words spontaneously and meaningfully at 12 months, his language development is rated *average*.

If a child is saying two words spontaneously and meaningfully at 8 months, his language development is rated *superior*.

If a child does *not* say two words spontaneously and meaningfully until 22 months, his language development is rated *slow*.

The Fifth Developmental Level of a child's language is *saying 10 to 25 words with 2-word couplets.* The couplets may be *big ball, red box,* or *Hi, Mom.* It makes little difference what the words are; he is on his way to stringing words together sequentially.

If a child is saying 10 to 25 words with 2-word couplets at 18 months, his language development is rated *average*.

If a child is saying 10 to 25 words with 2-word couplets at 13 months, his language development is rated *superior*.

If a child is *not* saying 10 to 25 words with 2-word couplets until 36 months, his language development is rated *slow*.

The Sixth Developmental Level of a child's language is *saying 2000 words and short sentences*. Short sentences come quickly, especially the "I want a" variety. The 2000-mark is usually reached when you find you can no longer count all of the words your child can say.

If a child can say 2000 words and short sentences at 36 months, his language development is rated *average*.

If a child can say 2000 words and short sentences at 22 months, his language development is rated *superior*.

If a child can *not* say 2000 words and speak in short sentences until 70 months, his language development is rated *slow*.

The Seventh Developmental Level of a child's language is *having a complete vocabulary and using proper sentence structure*. Now the child can ask any question and can express himself without being at a loss for words. The structure of his sentences is what we expect from others in our community. Verbally, he is now one of us.

If a child has a complete vocabulary and uses his words in proper sentence structure at 72 months, his language development is rated *average*.

If a child has a complete vocabulary and uses his words in proper sentence structure at 36 months, his language development is rated *superior*.

If a child does *not* have a complete vocabulary and does *not* use his words in proper sentence structure until 108 months, his language development is rated *slow*.

MANUAL COMPETENCE (*chart 7*)

The First Developmental Level of a child's manual competence is *grasp reflex*. Often mothers and fathers are proud of the grasp of their baby's hands when, at birth, the baby takes hold of its parents' fingers and does not let go. Actually, *releasing* the hand is a more sophisticated action than being able to take hold of it.

Chart 7: Manual Competence

BRAIN STAGE		TIME FRAME	MANUAL COMPETENCE
VII	SOPHISTI-CATED CORTEX	Superior 36 Mon. Average 72 Mon. Slow 108 Mon.	Using a hand to write which is consistent with the dominant hemisphere
VI	PRIMITIVE CORTEX	Superior 22 Mon. Average 36 Mon. Slow 70 Mon.	Bimanual function with one hand in a dominant role
V	EARLY CORTEX	Superior 13 Mon. Average 18 Mon. Slow 36 Mon.	Cortical opposition bilaterally and simultaneously
IV	INITIAL CORTEX	Superior 8 Mon. Average 12 Mon. Slow 22 Mon.	Cortical opposition in either hand
III	MIDBRAIN	Superior 4 Mon. Average 7 Mon. Slow 12 Mon.	Prehensile grasp
II	PONS	Superior 1 Mon. Average 2.5 Mon. Slow 4 Mon.	Vital release
I	MEDULLA and CORD	Superior Birth to .5 Average Birth to 1.0 Slow Birth to 1.5	Grasp reflex

The Second Developmental Level of a child's manual competence is *vital release*. Not only can the infant take hold of an object, but he is also able to let go of it. This is a life-saving device. Before, if he had taken hold of something sharp or hot, he would not have been able to release it.

If a baby has vital release at 2.5 months, his development of manual competence is rated *average*

If a baby has vital release at 1 month, his development of manual competence is rated *superior*.

If a baby does *not* have vital release until 4 months, his development of manual competence is rated *slow*.

The Third Developmental Level of a child's manual competence is *prehensile grasp*. Now he can pick up larger objects, such as a wooden block or a toy, by wrapping his hand around it, but he still does not use his fingers individually. It's as if he were wearing mittens.

If a baby has prehensile grasp at 7 months, his development of manual competence is rated *average*.

If a baby has prehensile grasp at 4 months, his development of manual competence is rated *superior*.

If a baby does *not* have prehensile grasp until 12 months, his development of manual competence is rated *slow*.

The Fourth Developmental Level of a child's manual competence is *cortical opposition in either hand*. In other words, he is able to press his index finger against his thumb, independent of his other three fingers. Now, by opposing his index finger to his thumb, the child can pick up objects.

If a child has cortical opposition in either hand at 12 months, his development of manual competence is rated *average*.

If a child has cortical opposition in either hand at 8 months, his development of manual competence is rated *superior*.

If a child does *not* have cortical opposition in either hand until 22 months, his development of manual competence is rated *slow*.

The Fifth Developmental Level of a child's manual competence is *cortical opposition bilaterally and simultaneously*. In other words, the child now can oppose the index fingers to his thumb on both hands at the same time.

If a child has cortical opposition bilaterally and simultaneously at 18 months, his development of manual competence is rated *average*.

If a child has cortical opposition bilaterally and simultaneously at 13 months, his development of manual competence is rated *superior*.

If a child does *not* have cortical opposition bilaterally and simultaneously until 36 months, his development of manual competence is rated *slow*.

The Sixth Developmental Level of a child's manual competence is *bimanual function with one hand in a dominant role*. Now the child can pour milk, sand, sugar, or even marbles from one cup into another. Here he is using both hands at the same time, co-ordinating an action.

If a child has bimanual function with one hand in a dominant role at 36 months, his development of manual competence is rated *average*.

If a child has bimanual function with one hand in a dominant role at 22 months, his development of manual competence is rated *superior*.

If a child does *not* have bimanual function with one hand in a dominant role until 70 months, his development of manual competence is rated *slow*.

The Seventh Developmental Level of a child's manual competence is *using a hand to write that is consistent with the dominant hemisphere*. In other words, if he is right-eared, right-eyed, and right-footed, he should also be right-handed. Again, it makes little difference whether a child is left-sided or right-sided, but both Doman and Delacato stress that a child at this stage of development should be consistent.

If a child is using a hand to write that is consistent with the dominant hemisphere at 72 months, his development of manual competence is rated *average*.

If a child is using a hand to write that is consistent with the dominant hemisphere at 36 months, his development of manual competence is rated *superior*.

If a child is *not* using a hand to write that is consistent with the dominant hemisphere until 108 months, his development of manual competence is rated *slow*.

The Doman-Delacato Developmental Profile is an extremely important diagnostic tool because it compares the child's abilities with normality. If a child, no matter what his age, is functioning at, let us say, Level Three in mobility, then our immediate goal is to get him to function at Level Four. Now we are looking at these children properly and are setting proper goals for them. We are not looking at a child's chronological age as a standard of pass or fail. Instead, we are looking at his neurological age and his present abilities.

One day, Glenn shows me a picture of a typical one-year-old standing with his arms in a balanced position—a typical toddler. Then he shows me a picture of an eight-year-old standing in the same position.

"Now, take a good look at those two children," he says. "First look at the one-year-old. Cute, isn't he? Taking his first steps weaving back and forth from side to side, but that's all right because his mother knows that soon he will be walking better. To watch that kid is a real joy for her. That's a kid any mother could be happy to have.

"But now look at the eight-year-old. He's exactly like the one-year-old, only he's bigger. He's an eight-year-old toddler — he's brain-injured. What is charming in the stance of the one-year-old is awkward in the eight-year-old. There's not any mother in the world who wouldn't be reduced to tears if she saw her child in that state.

"The real problem for that eight-year-old is that the

medical world sees him as an awkward, stumbling eight-year-old and decides that that's the way he is and that's the way he will always be. But they see the one-year-old and say, 'That's a great kid!' That is a tragic injustice. Because that eight-year-old is just as great as that one-year-old, but his time frames of development haven't been the same. Don't you see that?

"If both of these kids are going to be normal ten-year-olds, and that certainly should be the goal, then the eight-year-old has only two years to make it. But he has to pick up seven years of development in that two years. The reason the one-year-old looks so cute is that we know he has nine years, and we see no reason why he won't continue to develop year by year.

"Now, if we can accelerate that brain-injured eight-year-old's development so he can develop nine years in a two-year period, and as you know we do this at The Institutes all the time, doesn't it make you wonder why it takes that healthy one-year-old nine years to accomplish the same things? In fact, the one-year-old should be able to accomplish stages of development easier and quicker because he has everything going for him.

"We can move that eight-year-old up the stages of development because we structure his environment with intensity, frequency, and duration of stimuli. But the environments of most one-year-olds are low-key and not very stimulating. He has to pick up information as he can because adults have this insane idea that they have to keep secrets from him. Only when it's convenient for them will they stimulate his brain. And as you well know, it's rarely convenient for them because they have plans of their own. They keep him in a cage called a playpen — playpen, indeed — it's a prison of structured deprivation, and they surround him with the dullest pieces of nonsense. They repeat the dumbest things to him. That kid has to work to learn. He literally has to pry information out of them. It's a great sadness and a monumental form of insanity."

He sits down and reflects, "It's not the mothers' fault — they don't know any better. They don't mean to keep their children ignorant. They have been told to give their kids the cutesy, cutesy toys and to bore them silly with repetition. It's a great sadness — a tragedy."

I would imagine that most mothers who have read the preceding pages have made notes on which levels of development their child is at or how their child's progress compares with the *Profile*. I hope that you now have a clearer picture of the time frames your child has experienced and a better idea of what his developmental rate of speed was or is.

And I'm sure that many of you have jumped ahead and have started comparing your child's mobility with his language or his manual competence with his visual competence. Or you may have compared all six areas of development with each other. You may have found that your child's mobility is better than his language development or that his language is ahead of his manual competence. In other words, you may have found that in some areas your child is average and in other areas he is superior. And you may have found that in other areas your child is slow.

I hope that you have not concluded that that is the way it is because that is the way your child was made. I hope that you have not concluded that your child excels in some areas because his "talents" lie in those areas or that he is average in other areas because his "abilities" in those areas are average. And I hope that you have not concluded that your child is slow in some areas because your child is simply slow.

I would prefer that you have questions instead of conclusions. For instance:

Is my child's mobility average because our home environment offers him only average opportunities?

Is my child's language slow because his environment does not encourage him to speak?

If my child's language is superior, why is his manual competence only average?

And these may be the most important questions:

If I alter my child's environment from an average one to a superior one, would my child's development become superior?

If my child is already superior and I make his environment even better, will he become even more superior?

Since my child is already superior in mobility and only average in language, if I improved his language environment, could his speech also be improved?

And now that you've asked these questions, aren't the answers obvious?

Your child's development is not necessarily a result of his genetic makeup or his abilities and talents. In most cases it is a reflection of the quality of his environment.

Now, let me make several things clear. I am saying that by improving a child's environment, the child's development probably can be accelerated. That I *am* saying.

I am *not*, and I repeat *not,* saying that children should be in school at an earlier age.

I am *not* saying that the child should be pressured into learning.

I am *not* saying that you should buy a desk and chair for your child's room.

I am *not* saying that we should turn children into uncaring or unfeeling robots.

I am *not* saying that we should indoctrinate children into classroom regimentation at a very early age.

I *am* saying that young children have a tremendous capacity for learning, and they can learn almost without effort.

I *am* saying that young children can learn a great deal more if someone takes the time to show them the exciting things around them.

I *am* saying that young children will explore any environment. If the environment is exciting and rich with information, then the possibilities are great that the child will become an exciting individual and rich with information.

I *am* saying that if the environment is dull and lacking in information, then the possibilities are great that the child will grow up dull and lacking in information.

If you tell me that there are always exceptions, I will agree. But I will maintain that those *are* exceptions.

I will agree that it is possible that a child may not develop at an accelerated rate even in an enriched environment, because I know that there are such things as brain injury and physical conditions that can restrict a child's development (I must note, however, that I have seen hundreds of brain-injured children develop at astonishing rates once the environment was properly programmed).

Still, if you maintain that a slow child in an enriched environment is an exceptional child, I will also assert that that child is not nearly as exceptional as are the possibilities of a superior child's coming out of a dull environment. Not only do I believe that child to be rare, he is probably nonexistent.

Without the input of information, a computer is nothing more than a useless piece of machinery.

Without the input of information, a child is nothing but a living, breathing organism.

Unless a computer is programmed and in good running order, it cannot be expected to function at its fullest potential.

Unless a child is programmed and in good running order, he cannot be expected to function at his fullest potential.

If we do not respect the potential of a computer, then it is likely not to be properly programmed.

If we do not respect the potential of a child, he is not likely to be properly programmed.

Whether or not we love a computer, it remains a computer.

Whether or not we love a child, he still may grow with the years to become an adult. There is little doubt that if we love him and show him our love, he will become a better human being because of the affection we give him.

If we do not love our children and do not show them our love, then they become less than they might have been. Then we become less than we might have been.

15

The Missing Link

*"Intelligence is no human sideshow
but an evolutionary main event."*—
Robert Ardrey, African Genesis

IF we were interested only in statistics, and if we viewed children as interesting case studies, then we might become satisfied with our work and maybe even pleased with ourselves. But this doesn't happen.

In the late 1960s we still have two big problems with some of our kids.

Problem number one—oxygen.

We have long recognized that most brain-injured children are shallow breathers. They tend to have smaller than average chests, and they often have respiratory problems. We know that although the brain is only about three percent of a person's body weight, it requires about thirty-seven percent of the body's

113

oxygen. We desperately need to find a way to *grow* children's chests, increase their lung capacities, and improve their abilities to breathe.

Problem number two — walking upright.

We see literally hundreds of kids who, after they are able to crawl and creep properly, are then able to stand erect and walk properly. However, we see a significant number of children who cannot. We have to find a way to bring these kids upright. It should be mentioned that although parallel bars, walkerettes, canes, and crutches have been used for years in physical therapy, to our knowledge never once have these devices brought a child into a truly upright position. Those devices have encouraged the children to lean on something rather than to walk alone. The goal we have for our children is normality. If most of the other people in the world walked with the assistance of parallel bars or crutches, then we would allow our children to do the same. But the rest of the people in the world do not walk with such devices, therefore such goals are not proper for our children. We have to find some way to bring the children upright.

After careful reexamination of the spectrum of childhood mobility development, Glenn Doman begins to reason that perhaps there is another, *unknown* level of mobility between creeping and walking, a *missing link* in childhood development.

As he becomes convinced that there is a missing link, he also becomes convinced that we will not find it in medicine, psychology, education, or their allied fields.

Although modern science has probed the complexities of the human brain, charting its structure, chemistry, and functions, still nobody knows exactly *how* the brain learns. We believe that the nervous system of each human being must develop through a series of stages before the brain can function to its fullest potential. In effect, these stages of development repeat in telescoped time the evolution of Man, from lower forms to the unique human achievements of abstract thought, and speech, reading, writing, and language. We see our children duplicate the evolutionary stages of mobility development, from the level of the crawling salamander, through the level of the creeping quadruped, and then progress to walking on two legs with the hands in a freed position, which distinguishes Man from the other primates.

It is an established fact that at one stage in its development the human fetus has gills, and it is obvious that its intrauterine environment is aquatic. After birth, the infant continues through the evolutionary stages. We see the history of evolution repeat itself in each child's development. Millions of years crystallize into months. Ontogeny repeats phylogeny — the life history of the individual repeats that of the species.

Therefore, Glenn decides to turn to the field of anthropology for assistance. We go to South Africa to talk with Dr. Raymond A. Dart, Dean Emeritus of the Medical School at the University of Witwatersrand in Johannesburg. Professor Dart has long been recognized as one of the great anthropologists. He is the discoverer of Australopithecus, whose fossil bones proved that our ancestors walked upright more than a million years ago. Dart becomes so intrigued with our theories that he travels halfway around the world to join the staff of The Institutes in Philadelphia.

To find our missing link would have been interesting as an intellectual pursuit, but our search is urgent. Our kids are getting older, and they can ill afford the precious hours of waiting for us to find an answer.

One fact becomes crystal clear in our minds — our ancestors did not rise up from all fours on one bright, sunny day and decide to walk on two feet. They had to have had significant reason to stand erect and sufficient assistance and time to do so.

It is obvious that in order for our ancestors to stand erect, they had to hold on to something for support. What better support could have been available than a low tree limb? And what better protection from the predators than the refuge afforded by trees? There is an abundance of information to indicate that before our ancestors walked erect, they were agile tree-climbers. They developed the ability to swing from limb to limb, which literally straightened their bodies into an erect position.

If our ancestors learned to stand erect and walk by brachiating from limb to limb, Glenn felt it only reasonable to wonder if brain-injured children learn to walk by brachiating on an overhead ladder.

The results are better than we dared to dream. We see kids with bodies twisted like pretzels take hold of the ladder rungs and momentarily straighten with the help of gravity and the weight of their bodies. We see children who had been unable to open their hands, for the first time upon command, open their fingers and reflexively reach for the next rung. We have found the missing link—brachiation.

Until now we had assumed that when babies took their first steps toward walking, they held their arms up at shoulder height with their hands raised for balance. But now we know the truth. In all children's evolutionary histories and genetic memories there is a stage of development that has long been overlooked. They were reaching upward to grasp a branch that was no longer there. Toddlers lean on chairs and sofas because they are there now and branches are not.

So we place the "branches" within the children's reach. We instruct parents to build overhead ladders and to have their children swing from rung to rung. Children with mobility problems are assisted by their parents until they are able to brachiate on their own. Youngsters who are already physically active begin with short daily periods on the overhead ladder, and the time spent is increased as the child's strength develops in his arms and hands.

Since the inception of the brachiation program, many of the children who were previously unable to stand are now beginning to walk. Although this was our basic purpose for the program, we are even more enthusiastic about the by-products that brachiation is providing. Brachiation is helping to increase the lung capacity of these children.

On August 4, 1970, Roselise Wilkinson, M.D., and Evan W. Thomas, M.D., introduced our program in papers presented before the American Academy of General Practice, Ohio Branch, Columbus, Ohio.

In the 1970 fall issue of the journal *Human Potential,* a paper written by Dr. Thomas and Edward B. LeWinn, M.D., reports on the early results of the brachiation program. They state that of 547 brain-injured children in the study, 281 (51.1 percent) were below the tenth percentile of normal growth as listed in *Nelson's Textbook of Pediatrics*. Of the total group of 547 children, 426 (76.0 percent) were under the fiftieth percentile in chest circumference. Of the group of 547, 418 were measured on one or more subsequent visits over a period of 2 to 8 months. After the onset of the brachiation program, measurements showed a mean increase in rate of growth of chest circumference of 493 percent, or almost 5 times normal growth.

Now for the first time we are able to take brain-injured children who have grown at a slower rate than their peer groups and accelerate their growth to four and five times normal rate.

Due to the widespread professional and parental interest as to the results of The Institutes' work, in March 1971 the following facts are presented in a booklet entitled *What Occurred in Children Receiving a Program of The Institutes for the Achievement of Human Potential in Philadelphia, Pennsylvania?*

These children, who we diagnose as brain-injured, are frequently referred to us with a diagnosis that describes the symptoms of their problems, rather than the source of the problem. For example, a recurrent diagnosis is seizures or epilepsy.

The children in this group of 290 have been referred with the following diagnoses. All but the *last two* are symptomatic descriptions of the child's problem, rather than a diagnosis of the cause, which is brain injury:

Mentally retarded
Cerebral palsy
Epilepsy
Slow learner
Perceptual problem
Learning problem
Emotionally disturbed
Neurologically dysorganized
Neurologically handicapped

290 brain-injured children applied for and were accepted for treatment during the year 1968 at The Institutes for the Achievement of Human Potential in Philadelphia, Pennsylvania. The children are actually treated daily at home by their parents. Parents and child return no more often than every two months (and frequently less often) for reevaluation for the child and for the parents to learn a new program for the next two or three month period of home treatment.

Eliminated from the 290 children were 95 children who were under treatment for less than a year, since such children would have had, at the most, five visits and, at the least, no revisits at all. This was done because the staff is persuaded that five or less visits are seldom enough to give The Institutes' methods a truly fair trial. It is, however, interesting that in those children eliminated, two had been discharged as functioning normally, while only one had been discharged as a failure. Also eliminated were 25 children under 3 years of age. There were 270 children who met both the requirements of a year or more of programming and the age limit.

They ranged from mildly brain-injured children who walked and talked, but badly, to profoundly brain-injured children who were unable to move or to make sounds. Some of these were functionally completely blind or deaf. They ranged in age from 36 months to 17 and one-half years. The median age was 104 months. The mean age was 195.4 months.

Therefore, there was a total population of 170 brain-injured children ranging from mild to severely brain-injured and even comatose, at the onset of treatment .3 of these were traumatically brain-injured. Among the 170 children in the population, 146 highly important gains were made.

5 children have been discharged as graduates. 3 have been discharged as failures. Of the 114 children continuing under active treatment, 14 have entered regular class in school and 9 have been able to continue in their regular class placement.[6]

We are convinced that we are the most fortunate of men. Our goal is to make brain-injured children well, and every day our staffs—Glenn Doman's in the United States and mine in Brazil—are getting better and better at seeing that our children achieve these goals.

With so much success, one might think that we would begin ordering Cadillacs by the dozen and that other doctors from all over the world would come to us bursting with eagerness to learn. That is what one might think. Instead, a war is about to begin. We are attacked.

---

6. The Institutes for the Achievement of Human Potential: *What Occurred in Children Receiving a Program of The Institutes for the Achievement of Human Potential in Philadelphia, Pa.?* March, 1971.

16

Thank You for
Our Enemies

As I tell about all these important discoveries and
how it is possible to make brain-injured children well, perhaps
the reader thinks, "These men must be heroes."

One might think that in the field of medicine everyone
would welcome such innovations with open arms. One might
also believe in the tooth fairy and magic dragons.

In the last decade, The Institutes' methods of therapy for
brain-injured children have been highly controversial to say
the least. If Glenn Doman had invented a new chewing gum,
the world might have welcomed his invention with big smiles.
If he had developed a new deodorant, the world might have
responded with sociable armpits. If he had introduced a new
contraceptive. . . I leave that to the imagination of the reader.

Most people believe that the world is eager to accept new
ideas. But that is simply not true. It is especially not true in the
professional world. Medicine after all, is a profession, not a
calling as into the ministry, as some people try to tell us, and
not a charitable volunteer service, as most people who have

been hospitalized can testify. For the most part, medicine is a business, and most of the people who work at that business are professionals. They have all the virtues of professionalism and all the sins. They do not like their methods questioned, either by outsiders or insiders. If their methods are questioned, they quickly display their certificates, which proclaim them to be learned men with superior knowledge. However, if they make a mistake, they quickly maintain that they are *only human.*

I have nothing but respect for those who are eager in their search for new advances and those who regard their patients as living and loving human beings. I like to believe that these doctors are in the majority. I want to believe this. On the other hand, I have nothing but contempt for those who seal their minds and cannot see beyond their own egos. They are in the minority, I pray.

Sometimes I would prefer to mention that everyone in the world does not agree with our methods and then talk about something else. I think Glenn might prefer that I keep my cool. But then Glenn has the even temper and sweet disposition of an Irishman, whereas I am Portuguese, and my blood does not stay so calm.

If I don't say much about the controversy, then I am afraid people will think one of four things. One, that it was worse than it was. Or two, that it wasn't as bad as it seemed. Or three, that it still rages. Or four, that it no longer even smolders. All of these are false, and all of them are true.

I will explain.

It was worse than we wanted it to be because so much of the attack made on our work was based on hearsay, rumors, and malicious falsehoods.

It was not as bad as it seemed because we survived and eventually won.

The controversy still rages in the minds of the senile and those who are not aware of the work of the last five years.

And the controversy doesn't even smolder now in the

minds of the younger and more eager professionals who are replacing the old ones.

To put it as concisely as possible—opinions about our work have been diverse.

When the controversy over the methods of therapy for brain-injured children was at its height, those of us who were caught in the cross-fire realized that it was not a simple argument but an all-out war. On one side of the battleground stood the established medical and educational orders, and on the other side were the innovators.

In the April 1968 issue of *Archives of Physical Medicine and Rehabilitation,* an "official statement" concerning the Doman-Delacato treatments appeared. This statement was approved by seven voluntary and professional organizations in the United States and Canada, including the National Association for Retarded Children. Although these groups regarded it as an "official statement" of criticism, Glenn and I saw it as what it clearly was—an attack.

The news media immediately put the "official statement" into the headlines—"Patterning Without Merit!" Although Glenn and members of the staff wrote rebuttals to the attack, the newspapers that had splashed the criticism across the front pages later made only slight mention of The Institutes' refutation, usually lost in a lower corner somewhere beyond page fifteen.

Not only was it a war, it was an unjust war.

The principal criticisms were: (1) the system oversimplifies the problems of retardation and their solution; (2) the theory of neurological organization has not been scientifically proven; (3) The Institutes' treatments have not been subjected to large-scale, impartially conducted tests.

The Institutes has long sought a scientifically controlled study of the results obtained by their program as compared with the results obtained by other programs. As has been pointed out even by the complaining organizations, such studies are extremely expensive and difficult and would require many years of effort. The Institutes has carefully documented its many invitations to major hospitals, universities, and medical schools to join in such a study by providing the results of their own programs. To this date, no single group has accepted that offer. Many groups so approached have volunteered *other groups'* results for comparison. The Institutes still actively seeks such control results and herewith extends that same invitation to the organizations that have seen fit to issue criticisms.

That families must carry out the program of therapy 100 percent is hardly a criticism at all. I don't know of any prescription given to a patient with the instructions "take every other day, or on some days, or whenever the mood strikes." Of course the program must be performed as instructed if its benefits are expected.

As for the demands placed on the child, they are the same demands placed on all children—the demand of gaining the next level of development. The fact that in order for a brain-injured child to reach the next level of development he must have more opportunities with "frequency, intensity, and duration" does place more demands on the child. The alternative, of course, is to place no demands on him and let him stay the way he is.

There are those who question whether the home is the proper place for such therapy to be initiated. Some of these same people maintain that such a program could not be initiated in an institutional environment. The fact that this type of therapy is being initiated in hundreds of homes every day certainly attests to the fact that it can be done, and quite successfully, too. To my knowledge, Glenn has never suggested that such programs should or could be utilized in an institutional setting. On the contrary, he has stressed that the parents' dedication and concern are major factors in the success of such a program.

One of the strangest and most contradictory criticisms of The Institutes' work could be two distinct criticisms; but the two notions are so often repeated in the same breath, and out of the same mouth, that they sound like one—"The Institutes seeks publicity and keeps its methods and results secret." I have never heard of anyone's keeping a secret by seeking publicity.

Major articles about The Institutes have been published in *Life, Look, Saturday Evening Post, Reader's Digest, Coronet, The American Medical Association Journal,* and in all probability in every major newspaper in the United States. There are at least a dozen books that offer descriptions and explanations of the work. Carl Delacato has written five of these, Glenn Doman, two. It would appear that The Institutes' methods have had their share of exposure. However, I know for a fact that The Institutes for the Achievement of Human Potential has never sought publicity. It has never had on its payroll a person responsible for public relations. It has tended to discourage publicity rather than seek it. However, it has recognized its responsibility to share its findings with those who are interested. Glenn Doman has been cautious with the press, wishing only for factual and accurate reporting rather than exploitation and sensationalism.

It seems to me that with the problems facing medical and educational professionals, and with the problems facing state and national government in institutional care, that The Institutes' methods could be used to great advantage. These programs of treatment use the energies of the parents and the community in a combined effort to improve the functions of injured children. The thousands of parents who have initiated and maintained these programs are testimony to the fact that there is an army of neighbors who are willing to help.

One is led to wonder, after reading statistics such as "six million mentally retarded," "three percent of the nation's population," how the medical profession, the educational systems, and the national government can maintain a "wait and see" attitude.

As a parent of a brain-injured child, I realized a long time ago that a child cannot afford the luxury of "wait and see." It was only after ZeCarlos was placed on a program of therapy that he started developing. It's a matter of setting goals and having a plan to achieve those goals.

I believe in setting goals, and I believe that it is important that the goals we set for ourselves and our children are proper.

Constructing and maintaining buildings to house these children does not seem to be a proper goal. It has not proved to be a worthwhile accomplishment.

The goal of the staff of The Institutes for the Achievement of Human Potential seems to me to be a proper goal—to make each child a complete and functioning human being—to make him *well*.

"In a world that has thought this to be an impossible goal," says Glenn Doman, "it is not surprising that we sometimes fail. What is surprising is that, with increasing regularity, we succeed."

To listen to the past critics of The Institutes, one might easily imagine a mad scientist's laboratory hidden behind stone walls and a guarded drawbridge. There *is* a stone wall at the entrance to The Institutes, but there is no drawbridge and no steel gate. The doors are open to visitors, and it is a rare day when there are not several interested people being shown through the facilities.

Some of our critics call Glenn Doman a philosophical hothead. These people obviously have never met Glenn Doman, for if they had, they would be hard pressed to retain such a view. Glenn is one of the most reasonable men I have ever met. If the critics mean that he is unyielding and determined, I have to concur.

Some misguided people assert that there are no qualified medical personnel on the staff of The Institutes. One has only to review the qualifications of Robert Doman, M.D., Evan Thomas, M.D., Edward B. LeWinn, M.D., and Roselise Wilkinson, M.D., to be convinced that this is not true.

Often this assertion refers to the fact that the director of
The Institutes, Glenn Doman, is a physical therapist and not a
medical doctor. This is true. However, Robert J. Doman,
Glenn's brother, is a medical doctor and serves as medical
director of The Institutes.

Some contend that Glenn's charisma bewitches parents
into undertaking the mammoth task of rehabilitating their
children (as if it would be better if he were a bland gentleman
who spoke in a monotone).

Some maintain that Glenn is fanatic and uncompromising
in his efforts to make hurt children well. He is, indeed, fanatic
and unwilling to compromise for anything less than making
brain-injured children well.

The professional world does not seem to care whether
people are right in their innovations so long as the establishment is placated. To them, Doman committed the unforgiv-
able sin. Instead of offering his papers to the sacred Boards of
Education, he gave his conclusions to mothers. An unforgiv-
able sin, indeed!

Unless you have witnessed, as I have, the unprofessional
attacks of professionals, both openly and by sly innuendo,
upon a man whose sole purpose is to improve the lives of
children, you will not believe that such insanities are perpetu-
ated. For me, it has been like watching Galileo before the
Inquisition or seeing the sagas of Semmelweis and Pasteur.
The one thing that seemed to carry Glenn through these trials
and to give him renewed courage was that he was right.

In reviewing the biography of this man, I find it hard to
believe that, with his impressive background and list of creden-
tials, such emotional flames and professional animosities could
have been ignited by his innovations.

Glenn J. Doman, D.Sc., (Hon.) is Director of The Institutes
for the Achievement of Human Potential.

Upon graduation from the University of Pennsylvania School
of Physical Therapy in 1940, Dr. Doman joined the Department
of Physical Therapy of Temple University. He enlisted in the

United States Army as a Private on Pearl Harbor Day and served in the European Theater during World War II. He rose to the rank of Lt. Colonel. The United States conferred upon him the Distinguished Service Cross, the Silver Star, and the Bronze Star. Great Britain awarded him The British Military Cross, and Luxembourg presented him with the Croix de Guerre. Following the war, he directed the Norwood Rehabilitation Center until 1955, when in that year the Rehabilitation Center at Philadelphia was founded and he became Director.

During this period, he was Senior Language Consultant of the Chestnut Hill Reading Clinic, Member of the Educational Advisory Board of the Montessori System of America, and of the National Reading Research Foundation. For his service to children, he received the Roberto Simonsen Medal of Social Service to Brazil and the Brazilian Gold Medal of Honor. In 1966, he received Brazil's Highest Honor, the Knight Order of the Southern Cross. The Knighthood was conferred upon him in Rio de Janeiro by Brazil's Minister of Foreign Affairs. He is also recipient of the Statuette with Pedestal conferred by The International Forum for Neurological Organization.

By 1962, it had become clear that The Rehabilitation Center was destined to play a large role in enabling all mankind to achieve higher levels of performance than hitherto was believed possible on a wide scale. Under Dr. Doman's leadership, The Institutes for the Achievement of Human Potential was established.

Dr. Doman is President-General Emeritus of the World Organization for Human Potential, Chairman of the Governor's Committee on Human Potential for the State of Pennsylvania, and Chairman of the Human Potential Committee of the Pennsylvania-Bahia Partners of the Alliance for Progress. He is also the author of many scientific papers and several best-selling books for parents and children.[7]

If anything surpasses Glenn Doman's insatiable urge to gather more knowledge about children and how to increase

---

7. *The Institutes for the Achievement of Human Potential Board of Directors* booklet. Philadelphia, Pa.

their learning potentials, I do not know what it could be. He is a man compelled with fierce dedication. I have seen Glenn spend hours with a brain-injured child's family, viewing and reviewing the child's problem again and again until he finds a way to get that motionless child to move or that speechless child to speak. I have heard him in closed-door sessions with staff members and representatives from other organizations, refusing to compromise what is best for the children to gain either monetary or professional stature.

In 1968 Lindley Boyer, who was then an administrator at the Institutes, told Glenn that a certain medical organization had made overtures to accept the validity of his therapy programs if he would compromise some of his statements about the conventional treatment of brain-injured children.

"Oh, I'm sure they would," Glenn answered. "But then they always would have. It's because we haven't compromised that they see us as a problem.

"You know," he said, "it's like the story of Bernard Shaw, who walked up to a grand lady and asked if she would go to bed with him for one million dollars. Considering the price, she answered of course she would. Then Shaw asked if she would go to bed with him for one dollar. At this, the lady became indignant and said, 'Sir, what do you think I am?' Shaw answered, 'We've already established *that;* now we're trying to agree on the price.'

"It's the same here, Lindley. They're only trying to establish what we are. If we ever compromise, even over one line or one word, they'll decide we are whores and that we can be bargained with and that we can be bought behind closed doors or on the open market, as they choose.

"But there's something we must always remember — the knowledge we have gained and the methods of therapy we have devised don't belong to us, they belong to the mothers and the kids, because we could not have learned one significant piece of information or made one brain-injured kid one day better if it had not been for them. So we have nothing of our own to bargain with or to sell—unless, of course, we want to give away the rights of the mothers and children. I don't think that we're willing to compromise the children for one fleeting moment of acceptance."

Lindley nodded her head. "What shall I tell them when they call back?"

Without hesitation, Glenn answered, "Tell them to go to hell—they'll understand that."

I record this conversation not because it was monumental but because it was just the opposite, I tell of it because it was a quiet talk, away from an audience, that happened as Glenn and Lindley drove along Wissahickon Drive in Philadelphia. Who else would have known that a deal had been made, except of course, Glenn himself?

Since the world began, people have made mistakes about brain-injured children. These mistakes have not been rectified by modern medicine. They have only been obscured even further by clouded terminologies and professional rhetoric that define symptoms but do not diagnose the cause. In the last hundred years, if the only progress made was to stop calling brain-injured people *idiots* and instead call them *mentally retarded,* then surely the medical field has little to brag about and much to apologize for.

Sometimes I'm asked, "What happens if you see a child whom you think may be brain-injured or who may have a deficient brain? Do you ever see this kind of child? What do you do about him?"

Yes, we do see this child. And what we do about him often depends on the parents. It has always been The Institutes' policy that when there is an element of doubt, always give the child the benefit.

I've admired Glenn for this, because even in times when some groups were criticizing our work and causing trouble, adding pressure to our days and late hours to our nights, successes by numbers became important — not only to the children but to our survival. During that time, if there was one thing we certainly did not need, it was an additional kid whose potential for failure was suspected to be greater than that of the others. And surely the children who showed symptoms of having deficient brains had far greater potential for failure. However, not once, to my knowledge, did Glenn or any staff member set a higher price on a prestigious statistic than on the life of a brain-injured child. Before coming to The Institutes, ninety-nine times out of a hundred, these children had already been diagnosed as "incurable" or "hopeless" at two or three and sometimes as many as five state and private clinics. So in that respect we saw ourselves as the court of last appeal, and since we knew of no brain-injured kid who was brain-injured through a crime of his own, we always believed that he should be found innocent of having a deficient brain and be treated as if he were brain-injured until the evidence proved us wrong. Sometimes the child did not improve. But sometimes, to our surprise, the child did improve, and what a glorious victory it was. How happy it made us to know that we did not trade that victory for one percentage point of a statistic!

When one is fighting a long war, sometimes the war ends without anyone's noticing it, and the soldiers continue to fire at an enemy who is no longer there.

Twenty-five years ago, Glenn said that bracing the arms or legs of brain-injured children is ridiculous. Braces did not make their bodies more mobile. Most often braces made their conditions worse.

When we said that bracing was a bad thing to do, the medical establishment gave us a very bad time. They growled that that was a terrible thing for us to say. I remember accompanying Glenn one time when he said this in a speech. After hearing his charge, an occupational therapist jumped up in the back of the room, shook her fist in rage, and said, "How do you dare take braces off of these children?"

"Well," Glenn answered, "I guess that if you can justify putting them on, we can't justify taking them off. But if you can't justify putting them on, then we do not have to justify taking them off. The real question is not how do we dare take them off, but why do people like you dare put them on?"

She had never considered such reasoning before. She sat down quietly.

In 1970 I heard Glenn tell this story to a group of parents. Suddenly he stopped and asked, "How many of your children are in braces?" Only one couple out of thirty raised their hands. If we had asked that question eight years before, likely as not, thirty sets of parents would have raised their hands. (It's hard to believe, but we used to see brain-injured kids with no mobility problems who had arms and legs buckled inside rigid braces.)

In the past, one didn't have to have a brain-injured child to know how they were treated. The mass media and the public relations people conditioned the public. There were billboards on buses and trains and along highways asking people to give to United Cerebral Palsy or the Mentally Retarded Society. Always, always, always there was the most adorable, photogenic five-year-old child strapped in hardware from his ears to his toes. Every year the posters were the same; only the kid was different. The braces didn't change, except they always looked heavier and shinier. The whole world was conditioned to believe that braces were good for children with cerebral palsy or mental retardation.

After Glenn's talk with the parents, he said, "Raymundo, I want to show you something."

I followed him to his car, and we drove for about a mile. As we turned a corner, he pointed at a billboard and said, "Look."

I looked up and saw the new cerebral palsy poster with a charming little five-year-old girl.

"Don't you notice anything different?" Glenn asked.

I studied the sign. "No," I answered. "Except... the little girl doesn't have braces!"

"Exactly!" Glenn said. "Do you know what that means? It means the war is over. We've won. You know, of course, who took the braces off that little tomato, don't you? Not the Academy for Cerebral Palsy or the mental retardation group. We did! Not only did we take the braces off that little girl, but we took the braces off all the little brain-injured kids like her."

We sat and looked at the billboard for some time. It was such a nice way for those groups to surrender. It is so nice for the kids.

In the last five years, there have been other nice surrenders.

In 1971, Glenn Doman and I were invited as guests of honor to present our scientific views to the International Congress for Cerebral Palsy Society in Rio de Janeiro. We presented major papers for five days.

One might view the invitation as an apology. It was clear that the congress recognized that the work of The Institutes is extremely important, extremely advanced, and here to stay.

Like everything else, science and medicine and education have their styles and fashions. Recently we went through a period when acupuncture was scientifically fascinating. It was fashionable, and for a while it could do no wrong. In the case of acupuncture, it is obvious that science and the field of medicine were manipulated by politics — a ping pong team went to China, and suddenly acupuncture was a legitimate form of research. As a result, all over the world, patients were having needles stuck in their eyeballs, knees, ankles, and little fingers. Acupuncture is no more and no less scientific now than it was seven years ago, but seven years ago if a doctor had tried to talk about acupuncture in any medical group, he would have been dealt with like someone who had seven heads. This is no comment at all on the validity of acupuncture, just a remark about fashions and mores.

It is interesting that a few years before our presentation to the International Congress for Cerebral Palsy, many professional people all over the world had begun using The Institutes' methods of therapy—often under the guise of different terminologies and disguised labels. In truth, they were bootlegging the work. The head of some department in some clinic would prescribe crawling, creeping, and patterning as therapy but not tell the administrator of the clinic that it had anything to do with Glenn Doman or Raymundo Veras or The Institutes.

In short, in recent years almost everyone was using some of our methods, but they were pretending they were not.

At the International Congress, many therapists came up and proudly told us that they have done this. They thought we would be pleased to hear what they have done. We were pleased that they used our ideas, but we wondered why they weren't brave enough to tell the world or, at least, the heads of their departments.

People who use our methods and do not proclaim that they use them don't concern me so much as those who claim to do our work but don't. Because our names are becoming more fashionable, there are more and more of these people. These people say, "Oh, we know all about The Institutes' methods, and we know Glenn Doman as a personal friend." Often these people got our ideas from a book; maybe they met Glenn on a train or at an airport or have seen him on television. As long as we are fashionable, there will be many of these phonies. But if we ever go out of style, watch and see what Simon Peters they become. "I never heard of him." "What Institutes?" "Doman who?"

On June 1, 1973, the *National Association for Retarded Children* published the results of the Denton State School Study, entitled "Final Report—Sensori-Motor Training Project."

The Denton State School Study was initiated independent of Glenn Doman and The Institutes. In fact, the report clearly states that Glenn Doman had strong reservations as to whether such a study could receive a fair evaluation since the NARC was one of The Institutes' severest critics for many years.

The report clearly states that during the first three months of the study, The Institutes' programs were not maintained on an everyday basis. However, at the close of the study, the group concluded that the children who were on The Institutes' programs showed significant improvement over a second group given conventional treatment and over a third group maintained as a control in these functional areas: mobility and gross motor functions, visual perception, and language ability.

The report stated that results based on the intelligence-test data did not support a conclusion that the sensori-motor training caused general intellectual functioning. (It is hard for me to understand that improved mobility, vision, and language are not regarded as improved intelligence; however, the authors referred only to test scores.) The authors did admit, however, that the test scores were nonconclusive due to an insufficient programming to produce such effects.[8]

The report made two important statements:

1. . . . improvement in any one of the four functional areas would be regarded as a worthwhile outcome. To obtain results in three important areas appears even more impressive.
. 2. As a result of the Denton State School Study, it was concluded that the portions of . . . [The Institutes for the Achievement of Human Potential] therapy methods which were evaluated at Denton should be recognized as one legitimate approach in the remediation of certain handicapping conditions . . . visual perception, motor performance, and some language functioning.[9]

For the NARC to have initiated such a study and to have come to these conclusions renews my respect for the human race. The NARC's statements are clearly three things: a change

---

8. *National Association for Retarded Children:* "Final Report: Sensori-Motor Training Project." Denton School Study. June 1, 1973. Book 1, p. 9.
9. Ibid., Book 2, p. 65.

of mind, an intellectual apology, and a quiet surrender to truth.

The war is over.

We have won. But most important, the children of the world have won!

I have told you of these things because you may need this information. Perhaps you have a hurt child and you live in Wichita, Kansas, or Pineville, Arkansas, or Lonestar, Texas, or the Bronx, or Manhattan, or some other remote area. You take your child to the doctor, and he tells you there is nothing that can be done to help your child. You ask him, "What about the crawling programs or the creeping programs or the patterning programs?" He remembers some ancient hearsay. He does not know about the International Congress for Cerebral Palsy. He has not read the NARC study. He does not know about the timid apologies and the quiet surrenders. He does not know that the war has ended. You may have to tell him of such things.

In fact, your doctor's reactions may fairly well indicate how up-to-date he is on the subject of therapy for brain-injured children.

There are times when we become philosophical about our past critics. In many ways, they have done us a great service. They have made us sharpen our wits and strengthen both our resources and our people.

Outside my Institutes I have a large plaque placed by the front door for everyone to read. It says:

> O Lord, thank you for our enemies,
> because they make us stronger, and
> they have forced us to be brave.

Someday I will add a line to that plaque saying:

> And thank you for letting us win.

Part 2

17

Read the Directions
Carefully Before...

THE brain is like the earth. The earth is big but
the brain is bigger. The earth is one of many planets within the
universe but the brain is cosmic. As far as Man can reach out
into the universe so can he reach just as far into the brain. The
brain is not only information—it is imagination. It is both
precise and precious. It is both a storage place and a source of
information. It is both fact and fiction. Yesterday and today—
the past and the future.

Five years ago I could not have written this book. Maybe
even a year ago I could not have done this. While we were
being given such a bad time because of the advances we were
making with brain-injured children, it might have been sui-
cide for The Institutes and for me if I had even mentioned the
possibility that mongoloids might be made normal. If the
medical and educational worlds became upset because of the
simple truths we told about brain-injured children, it is not

hard to imagine what a furor might have erupted at the mention of *normal* mongoloids.

Perhaps even today reactions may be emotional.

However, I must now write of these things for three reasons.·

First — Our methods have become more fashionable, and the world has grown tolerant of us. No one is writing rumors in magazines. No one is charging us with heresy or immorality. No one is throwing rocks, either at our windows or at us. The peace is nice and gives us time to take a needed rest. However, too much rest is not good for growing minds and eager spirits. It's not good for the world to become set in its ways. Once in a while, it needs a little jolt.

Second — So many bad things happen to mongoloid children that it would be difficult for my conscience if I keep this information quiet any longer. Because every day these precious children are getting older and their lives do not become better. For them, I must tell these things.

And third — The years are growing shorter. If I am going to be the one to tell of these things, I think I had better not wait for some time in the future.

Again, I feel I must stress that if the reader has not read the first part of the book, he should do so before proceeding. It is not that I think you are not smart enough to understand the things I will tell you. It is that I am afraid that I am not smart enough to explain how mongoloids might be made normal if you do not understand the advances in therapy we have made with brain-injured children. If you have read the first part, then let us proceed.

18

The Last Days
of My Second Life

ONE evening in 1963, I am working late in my office. Although I don't know it, my second life is about to end. My third life is about to begin.

"Dr. Veras," someone says. I look up to see our accountant, Ary Nunes, standing at the door.

"Ah, Ary," I say. "How are you, my friend?"

"Very good," he answers, "and not so good. May I come in and talk with you?"

"Come in and sit down," I tell him.

He sits across from me, and I can tell that he is nervous. He is a nice man but a little timid.

"What can I do for you?" I ask.

"I'm sorry to interrupt your work," he says, "but my wife tells me every night that I must talk with you. I've tried to wait for a time when you're not too busy, but I've never found such a time. So tonight I said to myself, I better try now."

"Go ahead," I tell him, urging him to get to the point.

"It's about my daughter," he says. "We must have help for her. I've told my wife about the results that you've had with these poor children, and she says that's exactly the kind of treatment our Norma needs."

"Is your daughter brain-injured?" I ask.

"I think maybe something is wrong with her thinking," he answers.

"Have you taken her to other doctors?"

"Many times. And they say there is nothing they can do."

"What do they say is wrong with her?"

"Mongoloid," he says.

"Mongoloid?"

I look at his face and see my own face five years before. I hear the words, "Your son will be dead in two or three weeks." What can I say to this man? I know nothing about mongoloids, but I think they are hopeless. How do I tell him that?

I tell him, "Have your wife bring her to the clinic tomorrow." After he leaves my office, I write a note to myself— "Find out about mongoloids."

The following morning Ary and his wife Lolita bring their daughter Norma to the clinic. Norma is nine years old. I learn from her mother that the Nunes have a son who is normal and that Norma is the only mongoloid in either of the parents' families. I look at Norma and see the typical mongoloid face, — the open mouth with the tongue showing, very round face, short neck, very short fingers on her hands. Her body has practically no muscle tone. Her eyes are crossed slightly.

I notice that she is a very friendly little girl.

I'm not sure what to do with this girl. I watch her crawl— not very good. Her creeping is very poor. I see no reason why some crawling and some creeping would hurt her. I say to myself, "If I give these people a therapy program, it will keep them busy for a while and give me time to find out about this problem called *mongoloid.*" So I give them a program for their daughter.

They are so grateful that they thank me and thank me and thank me.

Every day the mother brings Norma into our clinic and does her program with her.

I start looking for books about mongoloids. I find that almost nothing has been written about them in the last hundred years. I learn little more than that their condition is called Down's Syndrome after the man who discovered that some of them have an extra chromosome. I think, "When I get to the United States, then I'll get some books on the subject."

19

"What Do I Do about Norma Nunes?"

When I get to the United States, I ask Glenn, "Why do we not treat mongoloid kids?"

Glenn answers, "Because they are not one of *our* kids, Raymundo. They are deficient kids, and our program won't solve their problems. Why do you ask?"

"Because my accountant has a little girl who is a mongoloid."

"I see," he says. "Too bad."

Then I ask Glenn if there are many books about mongoloids.

"Oh, I guess so," he answers. "Why?"

I tell him that I'd like to read one.

A few days later, when we are in New York City, we go to a very large bookstore, and I ask about books on mongoloids. I think that if I have enough money with me, I will buy all that the store has on the subject. When the woman comes back, she has only one little book in her hand.

I ask if there aren't any others. And she says that she is sorry, but this is the only one she has.

When I say it is a small book, I mean it is small in all ways — it is small in height, width, and length. It has maybe sixty-four pages. Reading English is slow for me, but on the train going back to Philadelphia I read all of the book. Other than descriptions, I learn nothing of real importance. The book tells me that mongolism is an inherited condition, that mongoloids are mentally retarded, that they die young, and that they are hopeless.

I finish the book and say to myself, "Oh, my God. How do I go back to Brazil and tell Ary Nunes and his wife that their little girl's condition is hopeless?" I suddenly feel like I am again running into the water to find ZeCarlos. I think maybe the other people on the train wonder why a grown man is sitting with tears rolling down his face.

Several days later, on the airplane back to Brazil, I reread the book even more carefully than before. I hope beyond hope to find that Norma Nunes is not really a mongoloid. Maybe she only looks like one. I make all kinds of wishes and many prayers.

The book tells me that mongolism is due to a chromosome abnormality and that there are three kinds of mongolism: standard trisomy, translocation, and mosaicism.

These are the kinds of things I read:

> Standard Trisomy: Occurs in one out of 600 births. The most common chromosomal abnormality in Down's Syndrome (mongolism) is Trisomy of chromosome 21. The total chromosome count is 47, instead of the normal 46. This type is rarely familial. Failure of the two chromosomes of pair 21 to separate during gametogenesis in the mother produces an abnormal ovum and thus a child with Trisomy 21. This usually occurs in children born to older women.
>
> Translocation: Rare. The abnormally large chromosome in

pair 15 is the result of the translocation of extra chromosome 21
material producing Down's Syndrome. The actual chromosome
count is the normal 46. In spite of this normal count, these
individuals have the same overdose of chromosome 21 as those
with standard trisomy. This type is familial. Children with trans-
location-type Down's Syndrome are usually born to younger
parents, one of whom carries the 15/21 translocation, The carrier
has a chromosome count of 45 instead of 46 but has the same
amount of chromosome 21 material as the normal.

Mosaicism: Very rare. Mosaicism in Down's Syndrome (mongolism) is the co-existence in one individual of cells with different
chromosome counts. For example, cultures of skin cells may show
46 chromosomes, blood cells, 47. The abnormalities may be less in
this type. This type is not familial. Mosaicism is the result of an
error in division of an early embryonic cell. One of the cells of the
developing embryo gets an extra chromosome 21 and passes it on
to its descendants. Thus there are two cell lines with different
chromosome numbers. [10]

I read that in 1865 a doctor named Lansdon Down ob-
served these children and made a list of how they differed from
other "mental" inmates. It says that Down's contribution in
diagnosing their problems was a major breakthrough and that
these poor children are therefore named after him. I mean no
disrespect, but I don't understand how his contribution was a
major breakthrough. What he offered was not a diagnosis but
simply another label, like mental retardation and cerebral
palsy. Down's Syndrome is not a diagnosis; it is a description of
the symptoms or the results of a medical problem. I do not
find that Down did anything to make these kids well; he merely listed the things that were wrong with them.

I also read about the physical and mental abnormalities
of these children. Or to put it in an entirely different way, I
read about mongoloid *normalities,* which is much like saying
that normal abnormals or abnormal normals or normals who

---

10. *Chromosome 21 and Its Association with Down's Syndrome:* The National
Foundation — March of Dimes, New York.

are abnormal but who, as a group, have certain normalities within the structure of abnormal classifications as compared to normal human beings, appear to be normal as a group, even when their abnormalities are admitted. (I write this only to prove that I can read and write in medical textbook fashion.)

It distresses me very much to list these things. I'm afraid that someone might open this book to this page and say to himself, "It's like all the others" and put it down. However, here are some of the major symptoms of mongolism:

Raised upper lip
Depressed nose
Strabismus
Speckled iris with normal retinae
Speckled iris with immature retinae
Epicanthal folds of the eyelid
Simian creases on palms of hands
Short and curved fifth finger
Wide spacing between the big toe and the second toe
Hyperflexibility of joints
Spinal curvature
Retarded thumb
High arched palate
Fissured tongue
Enlarged heart
Congested respiratory passages
Dry skin
Poor muscle tone
Premature aging
Delayed aging

These children have vision problems, hearing problems, speech problems, breathing problems, walking problems, learning problems. And on top of those, they have problems on top of problems.

I am sick when I read these things. I am sick in even

repeating these things because I believe such lists have made our doctors throw up their hands in despair and say *hopeless, hopeless, hopeless.*

At this point I think that I should remind the reader that I was for many years an opthalmological surgeon. I have performed thousands of operations. I have seen men's bodies torn apart by war. I have worked with severely brain-injured children and adults. In other words, I am not a medical sissy.

But I am a human being. I recognize Ary Nunes as a human being. I see his wife Lolita as a human being with a mother's heart and a mother's capacity for pain. And as I read this list, I see that all of these things tell me that their little girl Norma is not like other human beings and that the prospects are that she never will be like other human beings.

Should a doctor not cry when he realizes such things? Are tears unprofessional?

For once, I don't want to go home. As eager as I am to see my wife and ZeCarlos and Lourdinia, I know that with my return to Rio, I also must face Ary and Lolita Nunes.

On Monday morning I see Ary in the hallway and tell him I would like to speak with him later in the day. I see no reason to put off my unpleasant duty. Later that morning Ary comes into my office.

"Please," he says in his polite way, "before we speak of business matters, allow me to thank you for helping Norma so much."

I try to interrupt, but either my voice is too weak or he does not hear me.

"Before we put Norma on this program, she was so listless, like she was mentally retarded. But now she's more alert, and she's stronger in other ways, too. And for my wife, it's like a miracle."

"What do you mean?"

He hesitates and then says, "I was afraid that she was losing her mind. I didn't know her, the way she was. She wouldn't talk, and her mind was a million miles away most of the time. But now she wakes up in the morning and is eager to begin the day. Now she talks to me at dinner and makes plans for when Norma is well. We will never be able to repay you for your help."

I cannot find words.

"What did you want to see me about?" he asks.

I reach in my pocket and pull out a fistful of slips. "These are my travel expenses. Will you see that they're written down properly?"

He says he will. After thanking me once more, he leaves my office.

I decide to let them be happy for a few more days.

During the next few weeks, I find I can't sleep at night and my days are troubled. It seems that everywhere I turn my conscience is reminded. When I look at little children on the streets, sometimes I see mongoloids in their places. I see many girls who remind me of Norma and many mothers who remind me of Lolita. As if that were not enough, every day at the clinic I must face the real mother and the real Norma. I try to avoid them, but it's useless.

The child's mother tells me that Norma is much better, and I tell her that's nice. I'm so ashamed of misleading them that I cannot really look at her or Norma. Instead, I look for the first doorway.

One day Lolita sneaks up on me when I'm not looking. I turn around and there she is—her face looking up at my face.

"Dr. Veras," she says excitedly, "please come look at Norma and see how much better she is." Lolita takes hold of my arm so I cannot escape, and I let her lead me to the therapy room.

She hurries over to her child. "Crawl for Dr. Veras," she instructs Norma, and the girl begins to crawl across the floor. I am impressed—it's a good crawl.

"Very good," I say and start to turn away.

"Wait," her mother calls out. "Watch Norma creep."

I do as I am told and become very surprised. Her creeping is not perfect, but it is much improved. I look at Norma more closely. I notice that her muscle tone is improved, and her mouth is not as open as it had been before. I don't know what to think.

"I am very pleased," I tell her.

"Can we do something more?" Lolita asks.

"Yes," I answer. "Double what you are now doing."

"Yes, sir," she says without batting an eye.

Glenn Doman was right about parents. Can you imagine telling a professional therapist to double his work? He would throw up his hands and scream. But not mothers of hurt kids — you tell them to do more, and they're grateful. They are nice people.

During the next few months, I watch Norma more closely, and I see that she makes even more progress. Because I don't know any better, I'm not too surprised at this. In other words, I don't think of her improvements as miracles or anything like that, I just see the changes as welcome. And I think, "Isn't that nice for my friends?"

But the Nuneses do not let me stay out of trouble very long. Since they are so pleased with Norma's progress, they tell their friends, and soon their friends show up at the clinic with — as you have probably guessed — their mongoloid children. With some reluctance and much curiosity, I give them programs, and soon we have six or seven mongoloids in our clinic. We see them make similar improvements.

The programs for these children are very, very difficult. These children must crawl for four hours each day. They must creep for four hours. They are patterned eight times each day. They have eye exercises. We give them stimulation, stimulation, stimulation. The programs often take ten, sometimes fourteen, hours each day. It's hard work, but they improve.

We see their tongues recede into their mouths.

Their mouths close.
Their breathing becomes more normal.
They become more alert.
Their muscle tone improves.
They look less and less like mongoloids.
They look more and more like children.
They look less and less *hopeless*.
And more and more *hopeful*.

20

Three Happy Endings

I must now finish my stories so we can begin discussing how it is possible to make mongoloids normal. And I find that I'm fortunate, because I don't have a happy ending to my stories—I have three.

Happy Ending Number One—My Son ZeCarlos

The years have given me many pleasures. I see my little boy grow into a man. In 1969 he adds to my joy by graduating from medical school. Now there are two Dr. Verases. He joins my staff, and I soon see that he has initiative, a good mind, and great strength of character. With him, I see our work progress and the children improve even faster. I feel easier about the future because I know that the growth of The Institutes in Brazil no longer depends entirely upon my leadership and my decisions. Now I share the responsibilities and the long hours with my son, Dr. Jose ZeCarlos Veras.

Happy Ending Number Two—Norma Nunes

In 1970, after eight years of therapy, Norma Nunes, a former mongoloid, is now like a normal girl. She enters a normal high school to continue her studies.

Happy Ending Number Three—My Dream Comes True

For three years I annoy Glenn Doman and try his patience. Whenever I tell him that my mongoloids make very good progress on the programs, he nods his head like a martyred saint, takes a deep breath, and explains to me that mongoloids are not The Institutes' kind of kids. They have deficient brains.

This bothers me very much, though in all fairness I think I should say that this was when we were facing so much controversy about our work, and Glenn had enough worries about the survival of The Institutes. I think he did not want to consider embracing another bomb.

In 1971 I say to Glenn, "The next time you are in Brazil, you must see my mongoloids."

And he says, "Raymundo, I sometimes don't understand you. Are you still putting mongoloids on programs?"

I answer, "Yes, and I'm getting very good results. In fact, I'm getting better results with them than with other brain-injured children."

"Like *other* brain-injured children?" he exclaims. "Raymundo, you're like a brother to me, but honest to God, sometimes I think you don't listen to a word I tell you! Mongoloids are not like brain-injured children at all—they are *deficient* children with *deficient* brains. Everybody knows that!"

"I do not know that," I say. "I get good results, but, Glenn, you do not see. I think you maybe become like the medical world. You look, but you do not see. You hear, but you do not listen. What do you have against mongoloids? Are they not children? Do these children not have hearts? Do they not have names? Do they not have feelings? If you cut them, do they not bleed? And do they not have mothers—and do they not have fathers—and do they not have brothers and sisters? And are they not human? If they were hungry, would you not feed them? If they were hurt, would you not comfort them? If they had appendicitis, would you not operate on them? And if you would do all these things, then why would you not treat mongoloid children?"

When I finish, I realize that I have made a speech.

I stop and wait for Glenn's reaction. I think, "Oh my God, the Third World War is about to begin. Glenn Doman is about to declare war on Brazil!" I think my heart stops.

After a long silence, Glenn says quietly, "You're right, Raymundo. I have heard you, but I haven't listened. I have looked, but I haven't seen. My friend, I apologize. The next time I come to Brazil, I will both see and hear. If you have something to teach me, I will try to learn. However, if after I have seen and after I have listened, I am not convinced, will you please never mention mongoloids to me again?"

"I promise," I tell him.

I am very excited about Glenn's promise and become impatient for his visit to Rio. I begin to plan the things I will show him. I think I will start by having six mongoloids crawl for him. Then I'll have them creep for him, then brachiate, and then . . .

Then I stop and say to myself, "These things won't impress Glenn. He already knows that mongoloids can creep and crawl."

I walk over to the bookcase and take down *How to Teach Your Baby to Read*. I remember what he told me about Tommy Lunski: "I didn't need to see a thousand brain-injured kids reading to know that they could learn. All I needed was to see one brain-injured kid reading to know that all kids have this potential if they are shown the secret."

Then I know exactly what I must do. I do not have to

show Glenn an army of mongoloids to prove the point. I would show him one reading mongoloid. And not a twenty-year-old mongoloid or a ten-year-old mongoloid. I would show him Maria Teresa.

Maria Teresa would be perfect. She had been on a program for a little over a year. When her mother first brought her to us, she was a certified Down's Syndrome with a positive chromosome diagnosis and everything. And she still looked mongoloid. Her appearance is important for the demonstration since I don't want Glenn to think I'm trying to put anything over on him. And Maria Teresa is only *two and a half years old.*

When Glenn arrives, I meet him at the airport. On the way to the clinic, we tell each other the "best" and the "worst" and are soon up to date.

As soon as we enter the clinic, I take him to the room where Maria Teresa and her mother are waiting. I introduce him to this little charmer and her mother. Glenn is extremely friendly to them, but I think underneath he is a little concerned about this moment. That's all right—he's no more concerned than I am. If Maria Teresa could only guess how important she is at this moment to the futures of all mongoloids, I'm sure she would be nervous, too.

"Would you please read for us?" I ask.

Her mother hands Maria Teresa a book, and the little girl, without hesitating, begins to read in Portuguese.

I see Glenn is pleased at the sight. He smiles.

"Would you now change books?" I ask.

Her mother hands Maria Teresa another book, and she begins to read it with the same ease that she had displayed with the first book. The only difference is that the second book is in German, so she is now reading in German.

Now Glenn is absolutely delighted.

I gesture to the mother, and she hands Maria Teresa a third book. With the same ease, she begins to read in English.

Glenn is convinced.

Like me, he is not completely sure of what he is convinced, except that mongoloids are not dumb and that they are not hopeless. He is certainly convinced that they do not have deficient brains.

In December 1971 I stand in the auditorium of The Institutes in Philadelphia. The audience is composed of thirty sets of parents who have brought their children there for the first time. These parents look very much like the other groups I have seen in this room, but I know that this group is unique. All the people in the room are parents of mongoloids. For the first time in the history of The Institutes, a group of thirty mongoloids starts on programs of therapy.

My dream has come true. I have made a contribution to the work.

21

How to Make
Mongoloids Well

By now the reader should be aware that I do not believe that things have to remain the way they are. I do not believe that quadriplegics should become *good* quadriplegics or that brain-injured *children* should become brain-injured *adults.*

I do not believe that the proper goal for mongoloids is to become *good* mongoloids. Not only do I not think this is a proper goal, I think it is a lousy goal. It is a negative goal that threatens the child, because it holds more potential to make his condition worse than it provides to make him better.

When a mongoloid baby is born, it is not very far behind other babies in development. But because it doesn't develop as quickly as other children, over the months and years the mongoloid's condition becomes worse and worse. Now, it's a fair question to ask, Does a mongoloid develop slower than other children because it can't develop as quickly or because we don't expect it to develop as quickly?

Although I am not so foolish as to propose that our expectations are the only reason for his slowness in developing, I hope that no one would be so foolish as to say that our expectations for a mongoloid's development have nothing to do with his progress.

If we have a regular baby, and for some reason we believe that he will never talk and consequently we never talk to him, isn't it obvious that we will slow his development? Regular babies become regular children because of our expectations and the training we give them. That is so obvious that I do not understand why everyone does not see this.

Some may say that this is philosophy, not medicine. I say that such philosophy is responsible for medicine. If men had been content to let people lie in pain and die early deaths, there would have been no medicine. The field of medicine is the result of our not being content to accept that a person's health condition cannot be improved or altered.

But so many myths surround mongolism that when I say mongoloids can be made normal, people literally scream that such a thing is impossible. So you see, the main problem is that we are programmed to seek defeat with mongoloids. We have been told enormous falsehoods about these children. Let us take these falsehoods one at a time and see if we can bury them deep in the past.

Why are these children called mongoloids?

Mongoloid is a rotten label, one that is damning and demeaning. That man who, in the depth of his ignorance, first spewed out this term, spat it into our eyes and from that moment on, we see these children through his spittle. Because of our conditioning, we look at these children and nod our heads and say, "Yes, they do look *mongoloid.*" But they only look mongoloid to us because we expect them to look that way—they certainly don't look mongoloid to a Mongolian.

I am sometimes asked whether anyone ever examined the brains of Mongolians—the real Mongolians, who live in Outer

Mongolia — to see if their brains are different from normal people's brains. If such research has taken place, I am not aware of it, and I doubt that even the most naive researcher would seriously consider that these so-called *mongoloid* children have any relationship with Mongolians.

No one has ever proposed that all Mongolians are hopeless idiots.

But as unfair as such a statement would be to the real Mongolians, I am convinced that blanket statements and diagnoses of the little children who are labeled *mongoloid* are even more threatening to their futures. Fortunately, the real Mongolians live far enough away that they wouldn't even suspect that they had been labeled as mental defectives, and therefore they could live their lives with success and dignity, seeking their own happiness without answering such slander. However, the little children labeled *mongoloid* are not so fortunate — too often they live out their lives within the limits of its imposed impossibilities.

Do mongoloids really look Mongolian?

If you ask most people, "What do mongoloids look like?" they answer, "Mongoloids look different from us and sort of like each other and don't perform very well — and they look mongoloid."

Such descriptions affect our eyes in strange ways; we often see what we are told we are going to see.

A few years ago a speech therapist from Japan arrived at The Institutes in Philadelphia for a one-year postgraduate course. She stayed eight years to become head of The Institutes' speech department. She had a very clear way of looking at this term *mongoloid*. She said, "In Japan we have a group of children that don't look exactly like us — they sort of look like each other, and they don't perform very well. We call them *Americanoids*. That's a very fair appraisal because these children look as much Caucasian as they do Oriental."

If I showed the reader pictures of a Japanese child, a

Xinguana Indian child, and an Eskimo child and asked him to pick out the Japanese, he might pick the Indian or the Eskimo. All three look Oriental, and so in some ways they all look mongoloid. If I picked a Japanese who didn't look very Japanese and picked an Eskimo who looked very Japanese, you might decide that the Eskimo was Japanese and the other guy was Eskimo or Indian.

Now, we have examined Xinguana, Japanese, and Eskimo children for the symptoms supposed to be typically mongoloid — and we have not found any. Yet some of my own staff members have a very little fifth finger. We see people on the street who have epicanthal folds under their eyes. And when I look at my own right palm, I see that I have a simian line. I suppose if someone decided to diagnose my palms, he would decide that since I have a well-defined simian line on one hand but not on the other, I must be half mongoloid and half normal. Or half intelligent and half stupid. Or half successful and half hopeless.

Raymond Dart, one of the most famous anthropologists alive today, remarked to Glenn and me that if a roof caved in on a roomful of people today and buried them for two hundred thousand years, and if future anthropologists then exhumed the mass grave and examined the bones, they might conclude that different species had lived together in that one room. There would be one little fat one with a huge head, and one tall, lean one with a little head, and one medium-sized one with a medium-sized head, and so on and so on. People vary a great deal within this general anatomical structure we call human.

If we have grown to be so tolerant of big noses and little chins and fat stomachs and skinny legs, do we have to be so intolerant of these little children? Why have we made up names to call them? Are the names supposed to be complimentary? Do these names infer that these precious children are sweet and loving, or do these names infer that these little children are like foreigners?

Are all mongoloids alike?

There are degrees to everything. There are degrees of being athetoid, degrees of being autistic, and I believe there are degrees of being mongoloid. Some children are so mongoloid that one cannot miss recognizing them at a distance; some are so unmongoloid that one cannot tell they are mongoloid at all.

I have seen many good-looking, capable people with some mongoloid characteristics. For example, look at me. I am a very handsome man with a forty-five-inch waistline and a double chin, a capable surgeon turned avant-garde hero therapist with a simian line on my right hand.

Are the brains of mongoloids different from "normal" brains?

In some cases, yes—a little.

The human brain is divided into two hemispheres, and it is not connected until it gets down to the corpus callosum. In the operating room I could run my fingers between the two hemispheres. This separation has a certain importance to the function of the brain. In the mongoloid child, the separation is not so well defined.

If you look at the brain of a deficient child in the operating room, instead of seeing the nice, plump, spaghettilike convolutions that make up a well brain, you will see little, shrunken, hairpinlike microgyra. Such a brain is of poor quantity and poor quality.

In years past, it was believed that the brain of a mongoloid was deficient, and therefore its function could not be improved or enhanced. We believed this because the mongoloid brain does often look different from what is considered normal. What we were really saying was that if their brains looked any different from ours, then there was something wrong with theirs.

That's a very interesting attitude, which can be carried on indefinitely. If your nose is different from mine, there's something wrong with yours. This attitude has categorized, victimized, and ostracized mongoloid children. It is not only a great sadness—it is an insanity.

What should we call mongoloids?

Why don't we call them *children*? It's a more scientific diagnosis than *mongoloid*. I hope we soon learn not to use terms such as *mentally retarded, cerebral palsy, Down's Syndrome,* and *mongoloid*. If we continue using these waste-basket terms, it will be difficult to dispose of past misconceptions and ignorance. I am convinced that these labels describe symptoms and not causes. The cause of these ill-defined conditions is brain injury.

Is mongolism a medical term?

Medical labels, perhaps all professional labels, are powerful and at the same time limiting, because the public tends to believe that these labels carry some authority. However, could anyone think that *mongoloid* is a medical term or that anyone who uses it is truly a scientific person? Of course not.

If we say that *mongoloid* doesn't sound very scientific and ask the medical world to give us more information, the medical world answers, "We know, scientifically, that these children's problems are due to abnormal chromosomal patterns. We have chromosomal studies as proof."

We say, "Fine, we accept this. Now we understand. These children are the way they are because all of them have these strange chromosomal patterns."

But the medical world says, "Well, not quite all of them have these strange chromosomal patterns. About fifteen percent of these children do not."

Then we say, "Well, obviously that can't be the cause, can it? If a person does not have these abnormal chromosomal patterns, then he shouldn't be a mongoloid, he shouldn't have little folds under the eyes or any of these other symptoms that are considered uniquely mongoloid. True?"

At this the medical world stammers for a moment and then answers, "Well, there's a lawyer in New York who does not look mongoloid but who does have these chromosomal patterns, and there's a wholesaler in Denver, and there's a housewife in Portland — yes, there are some people who appear to be mongoloid and yet don't have these strange chromosomal patterns, and there are people with the patterns who don't seem mongoloid."

Then we ask, "Do you mean there are mongoloids who don't know they're mongoloids, and the medical world cannot prove that they *are* mongoloids by these chromosomal patterns?"

The medical world admits this is true.

Is it obvious which mongoloids have abnormal chromosomal patterns?

If we lined up a hundred children who look like each other, act like each other, and have problems like each other — who have little fingers, simian creases on the palms of their hands, raised upper lips, depressed noses, and epicanthal folds, and if we asked the medical world to pick out the fifteen children of the hundred who do not have abnormal chromosomal patterns, it would tell us they cannot do this.

We would then have to say, "You have developed a circular argument. Anybody or anything that does not fit your argument is not considered as a factor in drawing conclusions."

For instance, with this kind of scientific reasoning we could show that everybody lives to be 190 years old. All we have to do is throw out all the people who died before they were 190. Then we'd end up with everybody in our study living to be 190.

These children have been victims of such ridiculous circular arguments disguised as scientific studies.

Is mongolism a product of heredity or environment?

This, at last, is a proper question. In the past we have

been told that the problem is genetic. That would mean that the problem was present at the moment of conception. Conception is the moment when heredity and environment meet. Anything before conception is genetic. Anything after conception is environmental.

I think we must be careful in the terms we employ. If everyone agrees that *congenital* means those things a child is born with, then well and good, but let us not confuse *congenital* with *genetic*. *Genetic* has to do with the genes at the time of conception. The child spends nine months in the intrauterine environment from conception to birth. It is our custom to label a child's age from birth. The Chinese, more accurately, say that when a baby is born he is one year old.

I will agree that mongolism is a *congenital* condition since it is most often evident at the time of birth. However, I will not agree that mongolism is a genetic condition for there is no conclusive proof to that effect, particularly since mongoloids do not often reproduce themselves.

In recent years there have been studies in which researchers have tampered with pregnant rats and so produced a litter of mongoloid rats. In these studies, it became clear that mongolism can be the result of environmental conditions rather than genetics. At least this is true in rats. That doesn't necessarily mean the same thing would apply to people, but it's certainly a strong suggestion that it could be.

What is the major cause of mongolism?

I believe the major cause is prenatal brain injury.

What area of the brain is injured?

I think the injury is in the midbrain and the cortex, though I am not sure.

I know that the mongoloid brain looks different than the average brain, but then so does the microcephalic brain — it's smaller. So does the hydrocephalic brain — it's larger.

Surely our concern should be the material and the quality, not just the appearance. So if you ask me if I know, without question, that all mongoloids' brains are injured in the very same way or in the very same place, then I would have to answer, "No, I do not know this." And though I think those are important questions that require answers, I don't think that mongoloid children need to wait for the answers before they are helped. The most important question is whether we can improve the children's mental and physical conditions.

If we can change the mongoloid's conditions, then he moves out of the deficient category and into the brain-injury category, which is a much nicer and more hopeful place to be.

If you ask if I am positive that mongoloids are brain-injured in the classical sense, I have to answer, "No, I am not." But if you ask me if I am positive that mongoloids' brains are deficient, I'll answer, "I am almost positive that they do *not* have deficient brains."

If part of the definition of a deficient brain is that it cannot be helped, then I would immediately have to say that mongoloids do not have deficient brains. I do not have the slightest doubt that they can be helped — not the slightest — for I have seen their lives enhanced and their abilities improved. I have seen them enter normal school with normal children. I have seen them become normal people.

What is the cause of this prenatal injury?

It is our theory that poor nutrition is one of the major causes.

In the past we have been told that women over forty years of age are more likely than others to produce mongoloid children. This does not seem to be the case today. I see mothers of mongoloids who are in their thirties and their twenties. Why are younger women now having mongoloids? When we take a look at younger women, we see that cigarettes, coffee, Cokes, and hamburgers often compose their diets, even among the wealthy. It has nothing to do with money—it has to do with today's lifestyles. Add to the cigarettes, coffee, Cokes, and hamburgers the tensions women face today. Among older women, early menopause can cause endocrinological problems, and even older mothers today have become victims of poor nutritional habits.

And then take the study of a group of 1,000 women who were released from a concentration camp after World War II. The women in this study had four things in common:

1. They had all been in concentration camps for a considerable period.
2. They had all been starved for a considerable period.
3. They were all released and returned to good circumstances and good diets.
4. Four years later, 1,000 of them were pregnant.
   (By the way, it should be noted that the backgrounds of these women were as different as could be—some had been wealthy, some had been poor, some were Jews, some were non-Jews, some were French, some were Russian, some were German.)

So these women had nothing in common except that they were all incarcerated and that they all had poor diets for a period of some years. After release, they all had normal diets for four years. One-third of their babies were mongoloid.

We have known for some time that poor nutrition can affect brain function and in its extreme can cause brain injury. The children of Biafra were living and dying proof of this. Thousands and thousands of Biafran children starved to death—and of those who almost starved to death but lived, brain injury was present in almost every child.

Unquestionably, extreme malnutrition will cause brain injury. However, you cannot conclude that all brain injury is a product of bad nutrition.

I don't for one minute propose that I know what the main nutritional problem is that could cause mongolism. I simply propose malnutrition as a theory that accounts for the children of the women who had been in the concentration camps and that later may be proved to be fact.

Is mongolism the result of a brain injury rather than abnormal chromosomes?

Yes. I think the abnormal chromosome count is due to the injury instead of the injury being a result of the chromosome count. The abnormal chromosomal patterns are the symptom, not the cause.

Are all mongoloids in your program required to have a chromosome test?

In the old days we required that they did. Now we do not. These tests are very costly, and they tell us nothing of importance as to the child's potential or even his present abilities. We are more interested in improving the child's abilities.

Several years ago I became disenchanted with chromosome tests because they prove nothing. I see many children who look like the classic mongoloid but who do not have abnormal chromosomal patterns. I find mothers who have abnormal chromosomal patterns but who do not look or act mongoloid. Please, someone tell me what do these things mean? Certainly chromosome tests do not provide enough proof to count these little children out before they are given a chance.

What do you think of the new prenatal test?

This new test, called ammocentesis, was described at the 1971 American Academy of Pediatrics. To perform the test, doctors puncture the wall of the uterus and remove a small amount of fluid, which contains cast-off cells from the fetus.

The cells are studied for chromosomal abnormalities. If the fetus is determined to be mongoloid, such pregnancies can be terminated at the parents' option.

If this procedure becomes widely utilized, it has the potential of becoming the purest and perhaps the most efficient form of genocide the world has ever known.

If we had decided years ago that it was humane to kill mongoloids at birth, the problem could have been solved just as effectively. Many primitive tribes do away with children who are defective at birth. What is really the difference in killing these children before or after birth? Does it really become more moral? More humane? Or is it simply more legal?

What is the definition of a brain-injured human being?

A brain-injured human being is anyone with one or more dead brain cells. If I say anything else, I leave myself open to ridiculous arguments. For example: If you have 32,368 dead brain cells, you are not brain-injured, but if you have 32,369 dead brain cells, then you are brain-injured.

It is much clearer, much more positive, and much more scientific to conclude that a brain-injured person is a person who has one or more dead brain cells. And that is that—it is very simple.

What happens to the dead brain cells?

The body's systems slough them off, and they disappear. In speaking of dead brain cells, however, many people assume that you can go in and count them whenever you want—just open up the skull and say thirty percent of his brain is gone. This is just one of the queer ideas people (even some doctors) have about the brain.

What are the causes of brain injury?

We know of about a hundred different ways a child can become brain-injured, but there may be thousands. Some of the most common causes of brain injury are:

Prenatal — incompatible Rh factors in mother and father; glandular disorders in mother; German measles contracted by mother during first three months of pregnancy; lack of oxygen.

Natal — overmature prenatal period; premature delivery; protracted labor (eighteen hours or more); delayed birth (perhaps due to mother's late arrival at the hospital); induced labor; obstetrical difficulties.

Postnatal — childhood diseases such as whooping cough, chicken pox, measles, meningitis, scarlet fever, encephalitis, glandular imbalance, a blow on the head, drowning and revival, high fever, cardiac or respiratory failure during simple surgery, environmental deprivation, metabolic imbalance, and malnutrition.

Mental illness and brain injury are not the same. The mentally ill are defined as those persons who ". . . fail to adjust to society's demands. It is often because their mental disorders have caused them to lose touch with reality, or their emotions interfere with so-called normal response." [11]

However, brain-injured children can also have emotional problems, and because on occasion they have some of the symptoms of the mentally ill, they are sometimes inaccurately diagnosed.

How many brain-injured children are there?

Brain-injured children are everywhere. In the United States alone there are estimated to be over 6 million, which is not a conservative figure at all. It is an outdated, inconclusive figure. There are millions and millions of brain-injured children who are never labeled as brain-injured — millions! When you have been in this field as long as I have, you will finally stop being surprised at how many brain-injured children there

---

11. United States Department of Health, Education, and Welfare: *The Problem of Mental Retardation;* U.S. Government Printing Office, Washington, D.C., pp. 8, 9.

are. Then you will be amazed that anyone ever grows up without being brain-injured. And there's certainly a question as to whether anyone actually does.

I would not like to try to prove that everyone in the world is brain-injured, but I would rather prove that than attempt to prove they are not. I don't know how you would prove that anyone does not have some dead brain cells.

Doesn't the term brain injury frighten most parents?

It probably does, but it is not as frightening as *mongoloid* or *Down's Syndrome*. I think parents become frightened when they are not properly prepared to deal with such a diagnosis.

My first grandson was born in June 1971. He was born one month premature and was delivered by Caesarean section. When I first saw him, I knew he was brain-injured. A week later I thought it was time to talk to my daughter. I sat down with her and said, "Lourdinha, I have something to tell you." She looked at me very straight and said, "I know my baby is brain-injured, and aren't we lucky that we know what to do about it."

Immediately, we placed my grandson on a stimulation program, and he became completely well. He goes to school with normal kids, and no one has ever guessed our secret. He became a superior child because we expected him to be a superior child and we knew the things to do to make him a superior child. In fact, he is like a genius. My daughter was right — we were lucky, indeed!

Are the conditions of mongoloids hopeless?

I have spent the last sixteen years of my life — seven days a week, eighteen to twenty hours a day — living intimately with brain-injured children and their problems. I can never understand how some doctor can make the most devastating predictions about a child's life, and yet I hear such predictions time and time again.

Some doctor tells a mother, "Your baby will be like a two-year-old until he's seven."

Or, "He'll start having seizures when he's five years old."

Or, "He'll stop having seizures when he's eight years old."

Or, "He can't be expected to live past the age of twenty-one."

Or, "If he lives to be twenty-one, he will have to be put in an institution for the rest of his life."

I have not the slightest clue as to how people make such predictions. My opinion is that such predictions are complete nonsense, and I think they're extremely dangerous to the well-being of the child.

In the past, mongoloids have been victimized by reasoning such as, "Mongoloids are mentally retarded; mental retardation is an incurable disease; therefore, it is impossible to make mongoloids well." That line of reasoning makes me want to vomit.

That line of reasoning turned brain-injured children into mongoloids. It said to parents, "Your child is stupid. You must treat him like he is stupid and never expect him to be anything else but stupid." And if parents followed these instructions, they helped limit their child's potential, and soon the child developed into what the medical world had predicted he was going to be.

And when at last the child's situation became hopeless, then the doctors said, "Look, we were right."

I'll say it again—treat a normal child as if he were stupid—don't talk to him, don't take him out of the house, don't encourage him to play with toys, don't let him play with other children—and that normal child will no longer be normal.

Are mongoloids mentally retarded?

This is a question of false nicety. By merely asking it, one implies that mongoloids are not bright. Would one ask if

normal people are mentally retarded? Of course not. Then
why ask if mongoloids are mentally retarded unless one believes that the answer is yes. Well, it isn't yes. The answer is *no*.
Mongoloids are not mentally retarded about the world; the
world is mentally retarded about mongoloids.

When a mother asks me if her child is *mentally retarded,*
I have to ask her what she means by *mentally retarded.* As
we've already discovered, that term is ambiguous. Often it
means nothing more than *stupid.*

What is *stupid?* I am a medical doctor; I have perfomed
thousands of operations on people's eyes. Yet I can't fix a
faucet. If we have a leak in the bathroom, I call a plumber. In
Brazil, and I believe this is true also of the United States,
plumbers are not given medical degrees. So it is often thought
that plumbers are not as bright as doctors.

But it should be obvious that in the case of faucets and
pipes, there are many plumbers who are much brighter than
this surgeon. If the plumber should think that I am stupid
because I do not know about pipes, and if I think he is stupid
because he does not know about eyes, then we are both wrong.
Perhaps the greatest stupidity is to think such things about
each other.

It is the same with mongoloids. The gross stupidity is not
in *them,* it is in *us* that we have thought them stupid.

The truth is, most mongoloids are very bright children
who happen to be brain-injured.

Are most mongoloids in worse condition than other brain-injured children?

In many ways, mongoloids are often in much better physical and mental condition than many other brain-injured children. Mongoloids are not so crippled as athetoids. Their actions are not as repetitive as are the autistic child's. Their
muscles are not rigid, and in most cases mongoloids are very,
very bright children.

Do all mongoloids have vision problems?

I have seen some children who have vision problems that are not due to brain injury, but I have never seen a brain-injured child who did not have a vision problem.

Evidently, human vision is one of the most delicate and intricate skills, requiring a fine balance between the physical and the mental conditions. It seems that a disability in vision is the first and most frequent result of brain injury.

Can the visual competence of mongoloids be improved?

Yes. Most people do not realize that vision is a developed skill, not a God-given talent. Mongoloids often have a strabismus. The eyes do not move together. This is found in all babies at lower developmental levels. A good neurological program of therapy often improves this condition.

Can the visual competence of a mongoloid become normal?

Yes. I have seen this many times.

Since most of the symptoms are present at birth, is a mongoloid's condition easily diagnosed?

Yes.

Is an early diagnosis an advantage?

It can be a definite advantage today. I have some of these children on stimulation programs when they are only a couple of weeks old. We do not see most other kinds of brain-injured children until they are several years old.

However, in the past, early diagnoses were not to the advantage of the children. Sometimes the diagnoses were superficial ones instead of correct ones, and many children were erroneously labeled. Those who were correctly diagnosed were at that moment limited by the misconceptions that most people had about them.

These poor children were relegated to second-class status, and a special environment was created for them. I will call this environment "sensory deprivation."

These children were deprived of auditory, visual, and tactile sensation; they were deprived of normal learning situations.

Most often, it is this inadequate and abnormal environment that causes the mongoloid child to become an abnormal child.

Should parents be satisfied to let a child develop at his own rate of speed?

Only if they *do not* want him to become normal. The brain-injured child's best chance is his parents' dissatisfaction. Their unwillingness to accept his condition as unchangeable is often the only thing that saves the child's life.

I used to hear a lot about Freudian attitudes, such as "Don't be 'pushy' parents or your child will have emotional problems." Mongoloid children cannot afford emotional problems. When have you heard of a mongoloid with emotional problems? Let's make these kids well, and then we will worry about their emotional problems. It is easy to fix the emotional problems of well kids.

Do parents of mongoloids have emotional problems?

I hope so. I hope their biggest emotional problem is that they love their child. However, if that question means, "Do parents have psychological hang-ups?" then I would answer, they certainly should have. If they have a hurt child who is not getting better, and if his chances of getting well are becoming fewer and fewer and smaller and smaller every day, and if the parents are not psychologically disturbed, then something is very wrong with them.

Tallulah Bankhead once said that she was tired of people who used their psychological problems as excuses for poor manners. I love that thought. I change it slightly—I am tired of people who use their psychological problems as excuses for not reasoning.

Should parents have guilt feelings about having given birth to a mongoloid?

Why should they? What crime have they committed? As we get further away from the old genetic endowment theory and concern ourselves with the possibility of brain injury, then parents have less and less to feel guilty about—unless they smoke too much or eat poor foods on purpose. Even then, I hope we are moving away from superstitions and psychological gobbledygook.

Can the birth of a mongoloid baby have a negative impact upon the parents' marriage?

I usually see just the opposite. Mongoloids are most often extremely loving children. I think they are sometimes blessings to the family. I have seen them make marriages grow stronger.

I think the impact of such a child on the family has much to do with the family's view of what the future holds. If the future appears to hold nothing except failure and institutionalization for the child, then I see the family sometimes pulls away from each other.

But if the future holds hope for success and progress, then I see the parents join together and work many hours to make this child better.

Parents who do not accept their child's disabilities are sometimes told that they are being unreasonable. But you say they are right not to give up hope. Is this really realistic?

I think idle dreams are fairy tales, but setting goals and disciplining oneself to achieve them is a completely realistic approach to solving a problem.

But what if that goal is not achieved?

Then it is not achieved. That is also realistic. At least one can take pride in the fact that attempts to improve the child were made. I am convinced that no one in the entire world has ever been defeated until he decided that he was. I do not know why the world thinks defeat is realistic and that dreams of victory are unrealistic. That is a very negative attitude. I do not like it.

A mother recently said to me that her child's pediatrician told her that she should adjust to her child's condition and not expect him to get better.

I told her, "Forget that doctor; he does not believe in success. He believes only in failure. He does not believe in your child. Therefore, he is not worthy of the privilege of being your child's doctor."

Another mother said to me that her child's pediatrician told her to join a woman's club and to keep busy so she would not worry so much about her child.

I said to her, "You tell your doctor to join that club because it is your worry and your determination that provide your child with his only chance to get well."

**What is the greatest fear
that parents of mongoloids have?**

All parents of brain-injured children say the same thing to me—"What will happen to my child if I should die?" All mothers think of this. Only when parents make their children independent do they feel free to either live or die. Most people do not consider this, but mothers of brain-injured children know this to be true.

Should mongoloids be raised in a "normal environment?"

Isn't a mongoloid child a human being? Is his conduct any different from that of a hyperactive child, an uncoordinated child, or an undisciplined child? Why should the face of a mongoloid make us so uncomfortable? Are his actions so strange? Is he the only child who drools and holds his mouth open?

Is the mongoloid child the only one who does this?

Doesn't an autistic child have strange behavioral habits? Are we going to create a separate world for the autistic child, or for the severely brain-injured child? Must we create another world for the mongoloid?

Must we put them in cages? What crime did they commit?

Do they not deserve all of our consideration, our attention, and our loving care?

History provides us with a number of cases of children who were raised with animals.

In Italy we have two known cases of children of nine and eleven years who were found living with wolves. They were quadrapedal, living on decomposing food, and had the same characteristics and habits as the wild animals had. They were brought into civilization, and one of them died a few days later. The other survived for two years, always in an inferior condition. The child never succeeded in adapting himself to his new surroundings.

In India we have a case that is part of the world's medical literature. A child was found living among wild animals. Brought to civilization, he survived for two or three years, but he was always restive, frightened, and aggressive, like all wild animals in captivity. One day he was taken to the zoological garden and placed in front of the wolves with whom he had been raised. For the first time, he became calm and reassured.

We must draw some conclusion from these cases. If a normal individual is plunged into a wild environment and abandoned to his own devices before the full development of his nervous system, he will take from his environment his habits and his knowledge of life.

If this is so, how can we then create a special environment for mongoloids, autistic children, or brain-injured children?

These children, whose nervous systems are not yet organized, who have neither understanding nor normal behavior, cannot live in an error-filled environment. In creating such institutions for these children, we will make the mongoloid child more mongoloid, the autistic child more autistic, and the brain-injured child more brain-injured. It is time that the world woke up to this problem.

Animals are born with what we call chemical memory, what many people call instincts. We aren't. We are born with our nervous systems almost incomplete, immature, and without this chemical memory that passes from generation to generation. New-born birds already know how to build nests. Every species of bird makes a different kind of nest, though no school exists to teach the birds how to build their nests. Neither are there schools to teach spiders how to spin their webs. They have nothing to learn; it is instinct.

We do not have this instinct. We learn everything from our environment. The brain, will not, cannot, function if it does not receive instruction.

If we do not teach a child how to speak; he will never speak. If we do not teach a child to read or write, he will never read or write.

The child is the slave of his environment. His nervous system develops by use in an appropriate environment.

And if this is so, as we believe it to be, then it is unwise to separate the mongoloid child from other human beings unless we wish to make the mongoloid child an inferior creature.

What is a good neurological environment for mongoloids?

An excellent neurological environment is one that provides the child with magnificent opportunities to see, hear, feel, taste, and smell all the things that regular children see, hear, feel, taste, and smell.

A bad neurological environment is one that denies the child the opportunities to see, hear, feel, taste, and smell all the things that regular children see, hear, feel, taste, and smell.

A happy home, with loving parents who encourage the child to learn, is an example of an excellent neurological environment. Playpens, institutions, and other cages are examples of poor neurological environments.

Don't the programs of therapy you prescribe create an abnormal environment?

No. They create an *accelerated* normal environment. The child is not taken away from its mother and father. It is not removed from its home. We give it much sensory stimulation and much attention.

Why doesn't the mongoloid progress in a normal environment with normal stimulation?

Because he is injured. Like other brain-injured children, he needs *more*—more seeing, more hearing, more feeling, more tasting, more smelling, more mobility—more everything.

Is there such a thing as normal?

I don't want to play word games. When I say *normal*, most people know pretty well what I mean. When a mother says to me that she prays that one day her child will be normal, I do not ask what she means by normal. I have more than a good idea of what she means.

Like all children, mongoloids need normal opportunities. Normal opportunities offer chances for the child to learn about his environment, his home, everything that surrounds him, the usefulness of things at home, and the relations between these objects and the people of the house.

We must inform him about foods, daily activities, personal hygiene, and good habits. We should teach him to dress

himself and to know the days of the week and the names of the
months.

We must show him the beauty of things. We must explain
to him why birds fly and why the sky is blue. We must fill his
little hungry brain.

The mother of a normal child during the first week of his
life already speaks with her child for many long hours and
repeats, "Look at Mama, at Papa, at Auntie, at Grandpa.
Look at your little brother who is playing."

Why does she do this? This conversation is necessary
because this information will one day give the child the ability
to express himself and to reveal his thoughts.

The mother of a normal child must have enthusiasm. The
mother of a mongoloid child must have the same enthusiasm,
the same persistence as the mother of the normal child. And
one day she will have the great joy of seeing her child respond
to the information that he has received.

How much can environmental factors alter a child's intelligence quotient?

There is a well-known study of thirty-eight pairs of
identical twins. Separated in infancy, these twins were reared
in different environments. The geneticists Irving I. Gottesman
and James Shields found that since the twins were presumed to
be genetic equals, the environmental factor alone must have
accounted for a spread of fourteen IQ points.

If it is indeed true that environmental factors can alter
"genetic equals" fourteen IQ points (there are many who would
maintain that environmental factors can alter IQ thirty and
more points), then these classifications of mental retardation may not be static at all—they could well be musical chair
categories where an individual could be shuffled into and out
of a particular category depending on the medical, educational, and environmental help he has been given.

Surely it is possible to take a well child down through degrees of mental retardation in a matter of seconds with one precise blow to the head with a hammer. The question then arises, is it possible to bring a severely brain-injured child up through the levels of classification? If the Gottesman and Shields study accurately notes that environmental factors can make a difference of fourteen IQ points, then surely by that differential of fourteen points alone a child can be moved from one category into another.

Does an IQ score indicate the mental capacity of a mongoloid child?

An IQ score does not indicate anything except how well the child responded to the particular test or the particular tester. I hope that some day such tests are outlawed as insulting to intelligent human beings.

At The Institutes in Philadelphia and Brazil, we see many fifteen-year-olds who cannot read one word. They can't read the difference between *men's room* and *ladies' room,* the difference between *ice cream* and *poison,* the difference between *stop* and *go,* or the difference between *safe* and *danger.*

If these fifteen-year-olds are given a written IQ test, they score zero.

However, if many of these youngsters are given the same test with a tape recorder and allowed to answer the questions orally, sometimes they make scores above 130, which is considered superior intelligence. Now then, which are these kids—stupid or superior? Is it possible that a brain, through its eyes, reading, and its hands, writing, can register an idiot, while at the same time, through its ears, hearing, and its mouth, talking, it can indicate a genius? Of course not—one contradicts the other.

Most intelligence tests record oral or written abilities. The theory is that a child under six years of age will not be able to

read and a child over six will be able to read, so oral tests
are given to children under six and written tests are given
to children over six. If these tests are given to normal
kids, the test scores are reasonably reliable indications of
the child's abilities. If these same tests are given to brain-
injured children, they score not his ability but his disabil-
ty. Now there is nothing wrong in testing ability and there is
nothing wrong in testing disability. The great tragedy of
IQ scores is that although they test ability and disability,
it is purported that they measure intelligence. Nonsense.
That's like selling clay bricks as gold. Such procedures are
not only unscientific but dishonest. And they are dangerous—
they destroy children.

**When should parents create accelerated environments
for their children?**

If possible, on the day they are born.

The early years of the mongoloid's life are his most important ones, for it is during these years that he is learning and
developing faster than he ever will again.

Too often we see pictures of a mongoloid child sitting
down, looking listless and dumb. It's such a waste. If parents
make a stimulating and exciting environment for their child,
he no longer sits and looks listless. Instead, he becomes active
and more eager to learn. I know, because I've seen this many
times.

We often find that mongoloids do not do so badly during
their first years of life. In fact, their development is only
slightly slower than normal babies'. However, in later years, we
see the mongoloid's development become slower and slower,
and we see him become stranger and stranger. It is a fair and
honest question to ask whether the mongoloid would develop
this way no matter what or whether he becomes slower and
stranger because we not only *allow* him to but *expect* it of him?

I propose that it is the latter. Because we are told that mongoloids are slower, stranger, and dumber than average children, we begin to treat them as if they were slower and stranger and dumber, and soon they become what we have expected them to be.

How do you and your staff train the parents to do this therapy?

When parents bring their child to us for the first time, we see them for five days. The first two days are spent in evaluating the child's condition. We evaluate his functional levels according to *The Doman-Delacato Profile* (page 81). The next two days, we teach the parents about brain injury. And on the fifth day, we show them how to do the program.

It works very well because the parents not only know what they are to do, but they understand why they are doing each part of the program. I think this is very important. I think the best-informed parents do the best programs.

Do mongoloids differ greatly from other children you evaluate?

I do not like to talk in generalities because there are always exceptions. In fact, brain-injured children seem to be composed of exceptions. Obviously, we can see physical differences between the mongoloids and most of the other children. However, I should also mention that we see a physical difference between the athetoids and other brain-injured children. I think by now we are well aware of the physical appearance of mongoloid children and how they usually compare with the appearances of other children, so I shall not list these characteristics again.

We also see functional differences. When we evaluate a brain-injured child and mark his functional levels on *The Doman-Delacato Profile,* the top lines most often look like a picture of the New York City skyline. The child's Visual Competence may be at Level Three, his Auditory Competence at Level Five, his Tactile Competence at Level Four, his Mobility at Level Three, his Language at Level Two, and his Manual Competence at Level Four.

If we evaluated a child with a deficient brain, we would expect that all the levels of function would be extremely low and uniform — no peaks and valleys.

In evaluating a mongoloid child, we sometimes find that his functional levels can be indicated with two straight lines. One straight line goes across the Sensory side of *The Profile* (Visual Competence, Auditory Competence, and Tactile Competence). Let us say, for example, that this would be Level Four. The second straight line will be across the Motor side of *The Profile* (Mobility, Language, and Manual Competence). This line is usually one level lower than the Sensory. In this case it would be Level Three.

In other words, it appears that most mongoloids are able to take in information at one level of development higher than they are able to perform. They are usually one level brighter than their actions might indicate.

**What would the typical therapy program
for a mongoloid child be?**

Here we are into gereralities again. I will give you an idea of what a beginning program would be like. We would probably have the child crawl for three hours each day and creep on his hands and knees for three hours. He would be patterned five times for five minutes at a time. We might start a brachiation program. There would be eye exercises and tactile and auditory exercises. And, of course, the parents would teach the child to read.

How soon would you expect to see improvements?

In about two months.

What improvements would you expect?

The discipline would be improved. The child's eyes would be straighter. His muscle tone would be better.

How often do you reevaluate the children on these programs?

About every two months in the beginning. Later, perhaps, we see them at four- or six-month intervals. The scheduling of revisits depends on the child's condition and his progress. The revisits are never scheduled because of financial reasons.

Do mongoloids progress as well as do other types of brain-injured children?

They often make better progress than do other kinds of brain-injured children.

The typical group of brain-injured children develops at about one-third the normal rate.

However, the typical group of mongoloids develops at about one-half the normal rate.

So on the average the mongoloids are in better functional shape than other brain-injured children. Mongoloids are often at higher developmental levels when they begin our programs, and they usually respond well to the stimulating therapy.

How old should a child be before he is placed on a program of therapy?

The earlier, the better.

We see fifteen- and sixteen-year-olds achieve nice success, but I see the best results in children who begin the program at two years, one year, and better still, *one month*.

The mongoloid often has an advantage over other brain-injured children because his condition can often be recognized and diagnosed at an earlier age, and therapy can be initiated much sooner. So if you have to have a brain-injured child, in many ways, you are more fortunate if your child is a mongoloid.

Do you alter the diets of the children on the program?

Yes. Since many medical authorities believe that the difficulty in a mongoloid's ability to speak and function may be affected by a build-up of fluids (cerebral edema), we have the parents limit the liquid intake of these children. We feel it is easier to avoid putting in too much liquid than it is to worry about taking it out.

We also emphasize a high-protein diet.

What about vitamins?

We recommend Vitamin A and D supplements (oil base) and Vitamins B and E, which are vitally important for both the child and the family since they are all under a great deal of stress.

Are you familiar with Dr. Turkel's vitamin programs for mongoloids?

Yes. I have read his papers, and I have met Dr. Turkel. Dr. Turkel believes that vitamins are the best medicine for mongoloids. I believe that an *excellent neurological environment* is the best medicine for these children. Of course good nutrition is an essential element in an excellent environment.

What can parents do about their child's mouth being open all the time?

Function determines structure. I say we must get this child to be able to hold his mouth closed. The sooner the better.

Parents are often told that if they do not make an issue about their child's open mouth, the child will not leave his mouth open so much. Such advice is nonsense. If the facial features of a mongoloid are going to be altered, then we must emphasize that the mouth be closed. When the mouth remains open, the nasal areas will not develop properly, and the child's face becomes stranger with each year instead of better. Remember that function determines structure. Once we get these children to close their mouths and breathe through their noses, then their features change because we have altered the function of their facial anatomy.

This is not always as difficult as it seems. Some parents have only to say very nicely, "Sweetheart, close your mouth." For others this is not enough. Some parents have to be quite stern and touch the child's face when they remind him. And sometimes parents have to smack the child's lips, because some children require more intensity of stimulation than do others. With some children, parents use a variety of emphasis— sometimes only a gentle reminder suffices, other times a smack must be administered. In some cases parents have to tape their child's mouth closed for periods of time. Although this may sound barbaric, I can assure you that taping a child's mouth closed during periods of the day is more humane than allowing him to live his life as a mongoloid, scowled at by the world and considered to be hopelessly retarded.

Are mothers of brain-injured children different from other mothers?

At the beginning, no. But later they often change.

How do they change?

I think most often they become stronger. If they do not give up on their child, they have to be stronger—especially in the past, when they were so often told to institutionalize their children because there was no hope.

The mother of a brain-injured child begins no differently than does the mother of a well child. She expects her child to develop and grow. But the day her child is diagnosed as brain-injured, or labeled as being "mentally retarded," "cerebral palsied," or "mongoloid," she is often told that she must forsake her expectations. If she agrees to forsake her dreams, she is allowed to remain within the group called "reasonable mothers." If this mother, however, refuses to forsake her dreams and insists that she will find a way to make her child better, then she begins to meet raised eyebrows and turned shoulders. In the eyes of the professional world, she has become an unreasonable mother. If her husband stands with her in this decision, then he, too, is considered unreasonable.

**Aren't any of the mothers
you see ever unreasonable?**

I see many women who are unreasonable about women's things.

I see many men who are unreasonable about men's things.

But I see very few mothers who are unreasonable about mothers' things. It is not mothers who are unreasonable about the world. It is the world that is unreasonable about mothers.

I admit that I am prejudiced about mothers. And fathers. I like parents. They are so good for their kids.

**Do you perhaps place too much emphasis on
the importance of mother-child relationship?**

Absolutely not. I think the world is placing too little emphasis on the importance of the mother. The world has maligned mothers.

Several nights ago, I had a dream. It may have been an improbable dream, but it was not an impossible one. I dreamed that all the mothers of the world united and demanded and obtained certain rights.

First: When she gives birth to a child, a mother receives a diploma for enduring nine months of an expanded waistline and several hours of hard work properly termed labor. Pediatricians who wish to secure the child of a certified Mother as a patient must submit a written application and swear that they will make house calls even on bowling night.

Second: When the child is one year old, the Mother receives a certificate that proclaims she is an authority in regard to her child.

Third: When her child enters school, the Mother presents a report of her child's progress to go on record with every teacher's evaluation.

Fourth: At the end of each school year, the Mother issues a report card evaluating her child's teacher.

Fifth: When a psychologist releases his reports, a registered Mother has the authority to give him an ink blot test, analyze his answers, and wash his brain out with soap.

Sixth: As Mothers United, the group insists that every newspaper, magazine, and television station give space and time to display accounts of the good deeds and goals that humankind has achieved.

It was a beautiful dream. If such thoughts stagger your imagination, then it would be dangerous for you to try to conceive how the world would be changed if mothers united and put such a concept into action.

Are fathers important in these programs of therapy?

I speak so much about mothers because they are usually the ones who are more immediately involved with their children. I do not mean to imply that during this time the father is free to watch television or walk down to the corner bar.

The family unit is very important in this program. It may be considered old-fashioned, but I think it's a very old truth that a husband and wife should function as one person. The left side may be different from the right, but together they function as one. I do not believe it is possible for one parent to carry out this program alone. Both parents are needed.

**Why do you insist that the parents do these programs
with their children?**

I do not insist that parents do these programs. I think
everyone should make his or her own decision. In fact, I tell
parents, "This is a very difficult program. It will take up most
of the hours of your days. Think it over for a long time before
you decide."

**If the child is placed on one of your programs,
don't you insist that the parents are involved?**

I *demand* that they are, because parents are the best
therapists for their kids. I do not only believe this, I know it!

It is terribly important for the family to treat the child.
Sometimes wealthy parents don't understand this. They offer
to write a fantastic sum on a check and want me to take their
child and make him well. I tell them, "I do not need your
money, and I am not responsible to make your child well. This
child is a part of your family. I did not make him a mongoloid.
I did not make you wealthy. The only children I am personally
responsible to make well are my son and my daughter. If you
want to make your child well, I will teach you everything I
know. But I will not allow you to leave your child here. It
would not be fair for your child to work so hard while you go to
parties and have drinks with friends. And it would not be fair
for you to miss witnessing what courage there is in your child.
You do not insult *me* by offering me money—it is your child
you insult."

Aren't these programs very difficult to do?

Not in the sense of being complicated. Each part of the
program is relatively simple to do, so almost anyone can learn
how. What makes the program so difficult is the amount of
time and energy required of the parents. Some people say that
these programs are too demanding of the parents. I agree.

They are impossible programs. I believe with all my heart that no one other than parents could do them.

Why can't these programs be moderated?

The day that a mongoloid child's problems can be moderated, his program can be moderated. Is there anyone who believes that mongoloids have only a thirty-minute problem or a five-day-a-week problem? Mongoloids have a twenty-four-hours-a-day, seven-days-a-week, twelve-months-a-year problem. Parents know this. That's why they are willing to take on such a Herculean task.

Aren't these programs also very demanding of the child?

Yes.

Are the programs sometimes too demanding of a mongoloid?

Being a mongoloid is too demanding of these children. It is very difficult to be a mongoloid, and often very boring. We do not start a beginning program at full steam. We begin at the child's level of development, and as he improves and grows stronger, we increase the intensity of the program.

Aren't there medical problems that can keep a child from beginning one of these programs?

Usually the child's medical problems are the reasons he *should* be on the program.

Sometimes a doctor will say, "This child has a weak heart and must not do the program," or "This child has a kidney problem," or, "This child does not have strong muscles," or "This child's energies must not be taxed in any way because he is so delicate."

Let me tell you something. If even today, as a grown man, I suddenly stopped functioning as a human being — moving from one place to another and from one interest to another —

and became very lazy and sat around all the time and did not tax my energies in any way, it would be only a short time before I would become delicate and would have heart problems, kidney problems, and weak muscles. We must remember that function determines structure. These children's muscles will not become stronger unless they use these muscles, and these children's hearts will not become stronger unless they exercise their hearts.

Let me tell you a secret, a secret I cannot explain. I have seen people on crawling and creeping programs who began with very weak hearts or kidney problems or had cataracts on their eyes, and after being on the program for some time, they had healthy hearts, strong kidneys, and I have even seen cataracts disappear. I do not know how to explain this. Perhaps these are miracles. For twenty-five years I was an ophthalmological surgeon, and I never before made cataracts disappear without surgery. But I have seen them disappear after the patient has been on a crawling and creeping program.

I see these things, but I cannot explain them other than with the fact that *function determines structure.*

With such demanding schedules, don't some parents become exhausted?

Sometimes. When their children are on the program, parents work hard every day and find little rest. So every three or four months, I tell parents to leave their child with friends and take a few days' vacation.

Sometimes the parents say, "Maybe our friends would object."

I answer, "Then they are not your friends. If they were your friends, they would not see taking your child for a few days as a hardship but as an opportunity. What a nice compliment to give them, for you are saying, 'You are nice, bright people, the kind of people I want my child to know.' Now isn't that the nicest compliment you can give to anyone?"

What if there are other children in the family?

That's good. These kids can learn so much from brothers and sisters.

But what about the brothers and sisters?

It's good for them, too. They can learn so much from mongoloids.

What should you tell the other children about this child?

If there are other children in the family, don't build great barriers in their minds about their mongoloid brother or sister. Do not emphasize, in any way, that he or she is abnormal. Instead, emphasize the positive aspects. For instance, tell your other children that their brother's brain is injured and he needs the help of the family. He needs much information and much work. But don't fill their minds with black thoughts.

If your child had a broken leg or a broken arm, you wouldn't condition your other children to treat him as if he were going to be a cripple for the rest of his life. You would view his condition as temporary. So it is with your mongoloid child. If your family views his condition as temporary and treats it so, then it becomes temporary. But if you treat your mongoloid as if he will be a mongoloid forever, then chances are that is exactly what he will always be.

What one thing do mongoloids need most?

Discipline.

I cannot believe how some mongoloids are allowed to behave. Sometimes a mother brings her child to my clinic and within minutes the walls are shaking from the noise coming from this child's mouth. The child misbehaves, and the mother sits with a sad smile on her face and says, "What can I do? He doesn't know better."

I tell this mother, "Go home and teach him better and

don't come back until you do. I see pets that are better trained."

It is crazy to think that a lack of discipline shows that we love these children. Normal children must learn discipline. Why would anyone ever think that hurt children should not be restrained or taught how human beings are expected to behave?

How should parents discipline a mongoloid child?

With the same expectations and the same amount of reason that one would use to discipline a regular child. You must be consistent. You must be firm. You must be reasonable. And you must be loving, loving, loving.

When mongoloids are hyperactive,
do you prescribe tranquilizers?

When I hear mention of giving children drugs, *I* should take a tranquilizer. This subject makes me want to scream.

Drugs are not only a thriving business for the underworld; the drug business thrives in the offices of professional people. I see hundreds of brain-injured kids each year who are addicted to drugs. I refuse to call such prescriptions *medication* because I have never seen children made better by them. These drugs do not change the brain condition—they only hide the problem.

Giving these drugs to children who have brain dysfunction is like treating a broken arm by hiding the injured limb in a paper bag.

Three things happen to a child who takes drugs:

1) He often becomes more tranquil and easier to manage. He also becomes dull and listless, and in most cases this child, who *already* has a learning problem, finds it even *more* difficult to learn.

2) The brain-injured child's condition does not get better—it becomes worse because every day he is falling further behind normal kids.

3) The brain-injured child becomes more expensive because now his parents are paying not only for his "habit," they're paying in time lost with their child.

When parents bring a brain-injured child to my Institutes and I find that he is on a tranquilizing drug, I tell them that they must take him off the prescribed dosage.

Sometimes a mother will say to me, "Dr. So-and-so will be very upset."

I tell her, "I don't care if Dr. So-and-so is very upset. I care only about your child."

Then I ask her why she brings her child to my Institutes.

And she tells me, "Because Dr. So-and-so said his condition was hopeless."

And I ask, "Does Dr. So-and-so always prescribe drugs for his hopeless cases?"

You see, the answer is simple. It is not that I'm so bright, it is that the procedures are often so stupid.

I sometimes tell mothers to go home and take the little pills themselves. I know what will happen. A few days later, these mothers call me or come in and say, "I can't take those pills. They make me tired and dizzy. I can't get my work done during the day. Sometimes I don't even know where I am."

I tell these mothers, "Now you know what these pills are doing to your child."

After that we begin to decrease the dosage, and in time the child becomes unhooked.

What about drugs prescribed to prevent seizures?

I'm often told that these drugs are supposed to eliminate seizures, but I don't believe it. I think the drugs only reduce the overt responses to seizures. In other words, I believe the child still suffers seizures, but under the influence of drugs they are not so obvious.

The medical world knows very little about seizures. In 1968 a world-wide medical congress composed of leading neurologists and neurosurgeons from fifty-six nations convened in New York City to discuss the prevention and treatment of seizures. After three days of discussions, the only point they agreed upon was that they knew very little about seizures. They are not sure *what* seizures are or *why* seizures occur. They suppose that seizures are bad, but they cannot prove this.

I have heard that kids die of seizures, but I have never seen this. And every time I hear another doctor tell me how dangerous seizures are, I ask, "How many people have you seen die from one?" He always gets a blank look on his face and soon discovers he cannot remember seeing such a thing, either.

I think seizures do not do as much harm as we are led to believe. I think there is a strong possibility that seizures can be beneficial to the brain-injured person. I have often seen much improvement in a child's condition immediately following a seizure.

Now, if I'm asked if I want my patients to have seizures, I will promptly answer no, because they are frightening things to watch, and I am not sure what is going on inside the child. Nevertheless, I would rather take the chance of the seizure than have him so doped up he doesn't know his head from his elbow.

Should parents of mongoloids take their children out of the house more often?

Sometimes parents keep their mongoloid at home and avoid taking him along when visiting friends. This is a big mistake. How is your mongoloid child going to know what other people are like if he doesn't have the opportunity to meet them and be with them? Don't talk, talk, talk about his condition. The only important condition he has is that he is a child.

So, don't talk about his being a mongoloid. Instead talk about his being your child.

When people ask about a child's problem, how much should parents tell them?

Answer only what they ask. Never tell them more. Don't feel obligated to explain to anyone about your child. Don't be defensive. Every time someone asks questions, emphasize the normal conditions of your child, because if you don't, then you are perpetuating the idea that mongoloids are strange people. The public must be educated to the normalities of these children.

What should parents do if friends don't understand the problems of their child?

Some mothers say to me, "When I take my child into other people's homes, I sometimes find myself apologizing for his appearance or his actions."

I say to them, "Why don't you take him to the houses of your friends and leave other people alone? Surely you don't have to apologize to your friends. If your child had red hair, would you have to apologize? And if your child misbehaves momentarily, you don't need to apologize to friends. Just say, 'Boys will be boys.' I assure you, normal boys get into more mischief than do normal mongoloids."

Do you encourage parents to join organizations?

If parents want to belong to organizations and tell each other about their problems, that is their business. Such activities make grand pastimes for people who have nothing else to do.

Some parents tell me they feel responsible not only for their child but for all mongoloids, and they spend much time and energy supporting associations for abnormal children.

I tell them to leave those groups. The parents' first obligation is to their own child, not to groups of children. Their child does not have the time for parents to take on an entire world of mistaken ideas. Their child does not have thirty years to get well, or twenty years or even one hour. I tell parents, "Change your child, and tomorrow *he* will change the world!"

I hope the world will soon learn that too often organizations become entrenched in bureaucracy and self-perpetuation.

In April 1974 there was a small article in the *Philadelphia Inquirer* which, in its simplicity, related a damning truth. Obviously the article was not written by the Easter Seals public relations people. It read as follows:

> Eighteen years ago, Clare Jo Proudfoot was a cute, four-year-old girl on crutches charming millions as the national Easter Seal poster child.
>
> She had her picture taken with President Eisenhower and made personal appearances across the country.
>
> But she says now that twenty-two-year-old women in wheelchairs don't charm anybody. Out of work in Miami, she says she encountered prejudice from both employers and fellow employees in past jobs.[12]

This is a tragic article, for if this select girl, who for one year had so much publicity, can be so soon forgotten, it leads one to wonder what happens to all the little hurt children who remain anonymous.

I see these organizations not only in the United States but also in Brazil and throughout the world. They ask for money to open diagnostic centers, and many such centers open. But where are the treatment centers?

This tells us what the medical world believes about brain-injured children. They believe that these children must be

---

12. *Philadelphia Inquirer:* "The Scene in the Nation and the World—Update." Thursday, April 4, 1974, p. 3-A.

diagnosed as hopeless *earlier*. It's ludicrous. And if it were not at the same time so tragic, I would laugh.

When they are old enough to go to school, should mongoloids be placed in special education classes?

When the parents of a mongoloid child believe that he will one day become normal and begin to treat him like other children, then his chances of becoming normal are greatly improved.

The goal for our mongoloids is normality and nothing less.

When they enter school, we expect them to be enrolled in a normal classroom with normal children.

I do not want to see or hear of my mongoloids being enrolled in a "special" class. "Special" classes make "special" children.

Educators make big mistakes with "special" classes. Although they try to tell parents that "special" is supposed to mean "better," in their hearts parents realize that "special" classes mean "stupid" and that "stupid" children are put in "special" classes.

Mongoloid children are not stupid! They are not special! They are brain-injured children who need better environments and better stimulation. They should not be put away, out of sight and out of mind.

Not only do many mongoloid children have the potential for normality, but many have the potential for genius. Many of my mongoloid children read sooner and better than normal children. Many of my mongoloids are earlier and more proficient mathematicians. So I will not hear of my mongoloids being placed in "special" classes unless, of course, that "special" class is for *genius* children.

Do you believe that all mongoloids could one day go to universities?

No. I do not believe that all Brazilians will one day go to universities, nor all Russians, nor all Americans. Nor all normal people. The goal I see for mongoloids is normality. The day that all normal people go to universities, then I will think that all mongoloids should go.

This question should be, Do I think it is *possible* that any mongoloids can attend a university? The answer is yes.

Do you realize that most people do not think a mongoloid child can become normal?

Of course I do. A few short years ago I had some mistaken thoughts about this myself. I have learned better. Nothing bad has happened to me because of this knowledge. My left ear has not fallen off. My nose has not grown warts. Only good things have happened. It will not hurt people to learn of new ideas and new philosophies. In fact, I think it will be good for them. I know it will be good for the kids.

Thirty-five years ago, short of a God-sent miracle, a brain-injured child getting well was considered an impossibility. The majority today still believes this and says it's impossible. We know, today, that the majority is wrong. If the world says it's impossible for brain-injured children to get well and only one child gets well, then the world is proved wrong. From that point on, such negative statements are either mistakes or lies.

Do you think mongoloids should marry?

I think mongoloids should become normal and do all the things that normal people do.

Many times when I say that I expect my mongoloids to become normal, I see people smile and say, "How nice. What he really means is that he wants them to become *better,* or he wants them to be able to do *more* of the things that normal people can do, but he doesn't really mean that he wants them to do *everything* that normal people do."

For instance, if I say that I want my mongoloids to grow

up and work in factories, everyone says, "Isn't that marvelous!"
I do not understand this reaction. How is it "marvelous" to
improve children's abilities to allow them to become a cog in
an assembly line?

I say to them that when I say *normal,* I mean *normal.*
And they say, "We understand. You mean *as normal as possible,* but you certainly don't mean for them to *marry* and have,
well, *sex."*

I say, *"You fools!* Of course I mean that they should marry
and have sex. Why shouldn't they? Isn't sex normal? How can
we expect these children to grow to be normal if we don't
expect them to have normal futures? And certainly sex is a part
of normality. Sex is like breathing. It is biological, a necessary
bodily function. It is as much a part of the everyday as going to
the bathroom. To ask if I think that mongoloids should have
sex is like asking me if I think they should be allowed to go to
the bathroom."

Who do we think we are? Why do we think we have the
right to say, "It's okay if these kinds of people have sex but
those kinds of people may not." These kinds of attitudes not
only allow but encourage the caging and the segregation of
peoples. Hitler had this same kind of idea about the Jews. We
fought a great and just war to rid the world of such atrocities
across the ocean, yet we allow the same attitudes to thrive
undisputed in our own countries.

You may say to me, "Oh, come on now. You can't compare the institutionalization of mongoloids with the incarcer-
ation of the Jews!"

I answer, "Of course I do."

You may say, "You must be some kind of nut to make
such a comparison."

I answer, "You must be some kind of nut *not* to make such
a comparison."

You see, this is so obvious to me that I don't understand
why I should even have to mention it. Yet the world must not
understand, because we see these children placed in cages

called institutions—boys in one building and girls in another—
and the administrators predict that it is impossible for these
children to become normal human beings. Under such circumstances, wouldn't it be surprising if any of them *did* become normal? In fact, if we placed a normal child in such
conditions, could we expect that he would, in later years, be a
normal person?

If we taught normal children that sex was abnormal, and
if we guarded them during all of their lives and did not allow
them to marry, we certainly would not expect that they would
ever be normal adults.

It is the same with mongoloids. Mongoloids are people,
with a necessary biological drive that must be fulfilled. Therefore, sex should not only be an expectation in the mongoloid's
life, it should be a reality.

Do you think that parents will welcome these new ideas?

I believe so. Parents are interested in making their children better, so they are willing to listen, and they will try new
approaches. Besides, many of them have lost faith in the
medical establishment. They expect that more time and more
care be given their children. They also want answers to the
questions they ask.

It is not easy for the professionals to embrace new ideas.
In the past, professionals have had many mistaken ideas about
mongoloids, so many books in this field are wrong, and sometimes it is easier to accept wrong ideas than understand new
concepts. It is a new concept to attempt to turn mongoloids
into normal people. The concept is not difficult to comprehend if one's mind is not already bogged down with erroneous
ideas.

**Do many people still question the progress
of the children on your programs?**

Oh, of course. They want to see living proof. I don't think
pictures or records convince many people because they have to

read them carefully and compare them with other cases. Almost no one really wants to take that kind of time. They want to come to the clinic and be handed instant proof.

People come into my Institutes and say, "I want to see the progress of your children."

I show them through the rooms and say, "This child has been on the program two years and is doing beautifully. This child has just begun a program, I think in two years he will look better than the first child."

Often these people look but don't see what I see. They don't see either the past or the promise. They see only the present, and they think that it is reality. That's a big mistake, for the present is not a reality unless you are aware of both the past and the promise.

Sometimes I show these people three children. I say, "Here is Child A. He was programmed for three years, and today he is in a normal school and is like all other normal children."

Then I show them Child B and say, "This child is just beginning the program. He is very much like Child A was three years ago. With a lot of work, a lot of luck, and the Lord's blessing, in three years or sooner he will be like Child A and in a normal school."

Then I show them Child C, who has been on the program a year and a half, and I say, "This is what Child A was like a year and a half ago and what Child B should be like a year and a half from now."

I say to these people, "These three children are the same as one child — before, during, and after."

These visitors often nod their heads and say, "Yes, of course. We understand."

But frequently I see in their eyes that they do not understand at all. The different faces of the children get in the way of their understanding. *I* see that A, B, and C are as one child, but the visitors cannot see this.

What these visitors really want is for me to show them one

child. In the morning, this child would be severely brain-injured. At noon, he would be moderately brain-injured. And by late afternoon, he would be normal. And then, if the clouds open up and a golden light shines in the room, maybe they will believe.

Do you think that there will be great changes in the attitudes of professional people toward mongoloids?

I think the attitudes are already changing, not because they want to or are trying to but because they have to. All professions, whether they are medical or industrial or service or whatever, eventually have to respond to their customers' or their patients' demands. In the past, parents have been told that these poor children were hopeless and it was better to institutionalize them. As long as parents went along with that philosophy—and you understand that it *was* a philosophy, not a sound medical diagnosis — as long as parents accepted that philosophy, it existed. When parents began to refuse to accept such advice blindly and insisted on keeping their children at home, that philosophy changed.

Glenn Doman and his staff were major innovators and prime forces in changing the conditions and expectations of parents of brain-injured children. The things Glenn was saying fifteen years ago are now being accepted. Today, institutionalization is not only considered poor medical advice, but it is recognized as an unreasonable solution.

I hope it will be the same for mongoloids. Once parents insist that they want these children to become normal, then the professional world will be forced to comply. It is a new beginning.

And so, it will be as it has always been. It is the parents who are responsible for their children's lives. They are the caretakers of their days and the guardians of their futures. I thank God that it is so arranged, because parents have great love and great strength.

It is like Glenn said years ago. Parents aren't the problem. They are the answer.

22

It Is Time to Move On

WHEN I think over the last sixteen years, they pass before me so quickly that I cannot catch a single moment and hold it, either in my hands or in my mind. So many little scenes are now blurred into one overall panorama. I see the past as one views a motion picture running at ten times its normal speed. The overall images are terribly interesting, often entertaining, but once you have seen them the surprises are not so fresh, and it's time to move on to new sights and sounds. One must not stay in one place too long, or he becomes a part of the scenery.

In this book, I have told you many things. I have taken you on many journeys. We have gone into the Xingu, and we have probed deeper still into the jungles of the brain. We have walked where only a few have dared to step. I have introduced you to many interesting people. They are interesting not because they are my friends and my colleagues but because they are changing the world for children in positive ways. Their lives and their work have now touched your life, and, perhaps through you, your children's lives will be made better. I pray that this is true.

This book does not end with the last page, because now it is a part of your life. You will carry much of it in your mind and in your heart. It pleases me to think this, and I am honored to be in your thoughts.

For me, my involvement with putting these words on paper comes close to an end, but your involvement is just beginning.

If you are the parent of a mongoloid child, I hope that from this day forward your life will be improved and that your child will soon be normal.

If you are not the parent of a mongoloid child, I hope that you will see that this information reaches those who are.

If you are a professional who works with these lovely children, I hope that your eyes are opened to the potentials they possess.

If you are a mongoloid (and I fully expect that many of you will read this book), I hope that your life is rich with love, that your days are both eventful and meaningful, and that your future is limited only by your own desires.

Vamos! Tempo e curto!
Let us hurry! Time is short!

Afterword

A letter from Glenn Doman to his daughter.

Ms. Janet Doman   In Flight to Rio
301 Sky Heights Akasaka   18, January 1975
1-3-41 Roppongi Minato-Ku
Tokyo, Japan

Janny Dear:
    Your mother and I are en route to Rio.

    Try as I will, I can think of no other way to tell you—
Raymundo Veras is dead.

    And I am a little dead, too, and so to some lesser degree
are we all.

    I am, to a very large degree, responsible for his death, and
so to some lesser degree are we all.

    Perhaps with a little luck, (I am not sure whether good or
bad) I shall arrive in Rio in time for his funeral. I had started
to say in time to pay my last respects to him, but I shall never
do that.

In the end the death certificate will say some technically true nonsense as *acute myocardial infarction* or *heartblock* and that the time of death was *10:30 A.M. on 17, January 1975.* Nothing will be said about the things that stopped that noble heart. There will be no mention of twenty-hour-a-day schedules, of professional attacks, of personal insults, of silent tears, of forgotten promises, of physical exhaustion or of how many times that heart was broken. Broken hearts are not considered to be of medical importance and perhaps physical exhaustion is unfashionable this season.

I remember the day eighteen years ago when I first met Raymundo Veras and I remember the year that followed. I do not remember him for anything startling in that first year. It was, in fact, quite the opposite. I remember him as a quiet, mild, unpretentious man, who spoke very little English but who listened intently and who seemed to understand the *English* language.

As you know, Raymundo was *very* short and *very* fat. But he was in every way an extraordinarily strong man, from his towering strength of belief to the great strength in his face. He was strong of body as well. I have seen him, in bare feet, pick up ZeCarlos, when he weighed well in excess of two-hundred pounds, throw him over his shoulder as one would a baby and carry him a block, down a flight of stone steps, across a stone-strewn beach, and into the Bay of Guanabara. If it cost Raymundo any effort, he didn't show it.

I can't help but recall my first visit to Brazil. I was met at Galeão Airport by Dr. Veras and ZeCarlos and at least thirty of their friends. With them were an army of photographers, newsmen, television cameramen, and magazine editors, who had come to welcome the "world-famous Professor Doman." Until they told me, I had not the foggiest notion I was world-famous. At thirty-eight years of age, that certainly was a new idea for me.

It was love at first sight. I fell in love with Brazil. Just as quickly I fell in love with my new Brazilian friends and the greatest Brazilian of them all — Raymundo Veras.

In the days and years that followed, whenever he needed me to help with the children, I would go to Brazil — sometimes with only fifteen minutes' notice. And upon a phone call, Raymundo Veras would come to the United States when we needed his help. I remember when the president's father came to The Institutes after having his stroke; I called Raymundo to come help with Joseph Kennedy's therapy. He was so apologetic because the next plane did not leave until four hours later.

And so it was for almost twenty years. We exchanged ideas, we exchanged love, we exchanged people, we exchanged staff members, we exchanged patients, we exchanged departments. The only thing we never exchanged was money — not one single dollar or *cruziero* ever changed hands. It was the truest people-to-people campaign the world has ever known.

I remember Raymundo in -54 degrees Fahrenheit with his new friends, the *Skimoes,* during our trips to the Arctic. I remember how he loved the Eskimo kids. He couldn't believe we would have to go three miles by sled to get clean ice to melt for water when we were surrounded by snow up to our necks. This he learned only after he had used the water on the stove in our hut to wash his feet. When the Eskimo gal gave him a bad time, he told her that *Skimoes* were too clean.

I remember how we had laughed when the Brazilian Air Force had dropped us into the Capital of the Xingu Territory of Brazil to visit people a thousand years before the Stone Age, and the Xingu Palace Hotel turned out to be the only building within 800 miles and that it had a dirt floor and tin roof and wall boards with one-inch spaces between them, through which the beautiful and naked Indians watched us undress. They were particularly fascinated by our underwear, which was even funnier than our outer clothing.

I think of times out of mind when we had laughed and sometimes cried and saw children about whom we exulted and children about whom we had agonized in many countries and on many continents. I think of the times when we had marveled in our friends and had damned our enemies. I think of eighteen years and more.

Most of all, when I think of my friend, I see Raymundo Veras surrounded by kids, thousands of kids, all of them hurt and most of them mongoloid. I remember how he convinced us that they, too, had the right to be treated. I remember Raymundo — dear, gentle, strong, bullheaded, right, right, right, Raymundo. I remember my brother. Thank you.

We are now preparing to land at Rio. I will have to stop writing in a few minutes. Outside there is a driving rain and frequent flashes of lightning seem to illuminate the whole world. I can't help but wonder what now is going to become of The Institutes in Brazil that Raymundo gave his life to build. What will happen to The World Organization for Human Potential at which he served as president? What now will happen to the children of Brazil? Most importantly what will happen to the hurt kids and those that the world has called mongoloid and we now call the Veras children? How will their lives be touched by the loss of their fierce champion and their dearest friend?

Who can fill the shoes of this giant? ZeCarlos is barely out of his twenties. True, he is a medical doctor — a neurologist. Although he is no longer a quadriplegic, he still requires a wheelchair to get about. But he is still a boy. How can one expect a boy to take the place of a king?

His father was a gentleman and a gentle man in the old world cast who learned to become a brawler and a streetfighter when it was necessary to defend his children. He was truly a king with a crown on his head and a club in his hand. ZeCarlos is no streetfighter or brawler. He is gentler — a more serious and quiet person, more like his father was when I first knew him. But his father grew to be a warrior. He never shied away from battle even when he would rather not fight. In the last years, when confrontations were inevitable, a certain flat look would come across his face much like I imagine the Spartans must have looked. I have never seen this look on the face of ZeCarlos. I don't know if such a look is even possible for him.

So who will carry on his father's work — the directors of the other Institutes in Brazil? They are all good men and capable physicians, and they are older than ZeCarlos. But they are not kings. I am not sure that they are even warriors. Perhaps they will be someday, but not now. And the need is now.

The most immediate need is to determine who will serve out the term of president of the World Organization until the end of May when the annual meeting will be held. The vice-president at large is unable to take over this responsibility until then. As the only living past president, it falls upon me to appoint an interim president.

As you can see, I have many questions in search of answers. We are about to land. I have to buckle my seat belt.

> In Flight to Philadelphia
> 20, January 1975

Your mother and I arrived too late to attend Raymundo's funeral. Yesterday ZeCarlos and his wife, Concepcão, picked us up at our hotel and asked us where we would like to go. We visited the hospital where Raymundo Veras had been a successful opthalmological surgeon and where he spent his final hours.

And then we went to the cemetery in downtown Rio. Standing by the site of the freshly dug grave, I had none of the feelings of horror and despair that such places usually trigger in me. It was much too soon to miss Raymundo. I felt instead a strong sense of historical impact and a very personal sense of saying so long to my friend and my brother.

ZeCarlos told us that his father had requested that his body remain in Rio for five years and then he wished to be returned to Ceara, where he was born. Your mother and I agreed to return in five years and take Raymundo home.

Then we drove to The Institutes and visited Raymundo's office. It was exactly as he had left it. His desk was piled high with children's medical charts, journals of medicine and other fields, and several pair of glasses. As you know he often misplaced them.

In the center of the desktop, there were three letters from me. They had all been opened and returned to their envelopes. His pen was in position, as if he were about to write a personal letter.

We decided that his office should be left exactly as it was. When we left, we locked the room. It will become The Raymundo Veras Office Museum to be undisturbed throughout all time.

This morning I realized I had to put my grief aside and find answers for my questions. ZeCarlos and I talked. I explained to him that although this was a difficult time for him, we had to make some decisions. First things first — I asked him to act as Interim President of the World Organization of Human Potential in his father's place until the constitutional convention May 10.

"Do you believe that I can do this?" he asked quietly.

"I believe you *must*," I answered carefully.

"Then I *will*," he answered firmly.

"Now, ZeCarlos," I said, "as painful as it may be, I believe it is necessary for you to immediately call a meeting of all the South American medical directors and select the chief director. Not one moment must be wasted for the treatment of the children."

"Yes, I know," he answered. "I have already done this."

"When is the meeting scheduled?"

"Two days ago. After my father's funeral," he said.

"And who was named chief director?" I wanted to know.

"I was."

"And the older doctors agreed?" I asked.

"There was much talk, but in the end, they agreed," he said. "It will be okay. You will see."

I suddenly found myself looking at this young man differently. Obviously he was no longer a boy.

"ZeCarlos," I said, "I told your mother and Lourdinha that I more than anyone else was responsible for your father's death. They didn't deny this."

"In some ways, Glenn, this is true, but my father knew what he was doing. He would not have had it otherwise."

"I accept that responsibility," I told him, "but I'm not prepared to add you to my conscience."

"This is not your decision," he replied. "It is mine."

"But there are still many battles. There are still many who oppose our work."

"Not as many as there used to be," he said. "The world is changing and gradually accepting our methods. The opposition is not as strong as it was for you and my father."

"But there will still be attacks," I told him. "They will attack you both professionally and personally. How will you answer them?"

"I will answer them more softly than my father did. By living his life, he has made mine easier."

"But some of them will try to destroy you. What will you do when your soft answers will no longer work?"

"I will send them to hell."

Rather presumptuously, I corrected his English. "You mean that you will tell them to *go* to hell."

"No, Glenn," he said firmly, "I know what I am saying. I will *send* them to hell."

I looked at his face. It had a rather flat expression—like a Spartan. For a moment, I thought I was sitting with his father. It was a curious feeling indeed.

Several times on the way to the airport, I found myself calling him Raymundo. And I noticed that your mother corrected herself a couple of times. I have never before understood the English expression, "The king is dead—long live the king." Your mother said that she always has, but as you know, she has always been several steps ahead of me. But now, for the first time, I understand it.

I remember last May, before Raymundo and I left for Ireland, I asked him, "Have you ever wondered what would happen to our work if something happened to either of us?"

"There is no need to worry," he said. "You have a good staff to carry on and I am leaving a legacy."

At the time I thought the legacy Raymundo was referring to was his staff. But now I know better. His legacy is his son, Dr. José Carlos Veras.

I am grateful for his legacy and I will treasure his gift. I am sure that in years to come the hurt children of Brazil, and indeed, the hurt children throughout the world, will benefit from the dedication and leadership of this young man—Raymundo's son. I look forward to the future and this new generation.

Still, in my heart, I know there will never be another Raymundo Veras. I shall miss him. I shall miss him very much.

All our love,
Mom and Dad